Summer at the Lake of Monteith

SUMMER

AT THE

LAKE OF MONTEITH.

BY P. DUN,

STATION MASTER, PORT OF MONTEITH.

SECOND EDITION.

EDINBURGH: OLIVER AND BOYD.
GLASGOW: DAVID ROBERTSON.
STIRLING: ALEXANDER MILLER.
AND ALL BOOKSELLERS.
MDCCCLXVII.

GLASGOW: PRINTED BY JAMES HEDDERWICK AND SON,
Printers to the Queen.

TO

MR. AND MRS. ERSKINE,

OF CARDROSS,

THESE PAGES ARE, WITH THE MOST PERFECT RESPECT,
INSCRIBED

BY

THE AUTHOR.

PREFACE.

THESE pages—containing some notes of a locality unsurpassed in placid loveliness, and surrounded by much of the sublime, but which has hitherto attracted little notice of the great travelling world—are now, for the first time, presented to the public in a collected form.

When the idea first occurred to the Author, of bringing the "Lake of Monteith," and the old traditions that still linger around its shores, prominently before the public, he was actuated by the desire of lending his humble aid to raise in the estimation of those who, flying from the din and bustle of commerce, seek for health and pleasure amid the glories of Nature, a locality which, although seldom traversed by the tourists who flock from all quarters of the world to behold with their own eyes the land of "the mountain and the flood," is, in his estimation, unrivalled in its varied charms, and to which he feels proud to be united by the strong tie of nativity. In attempting this, however, he acknowledges his inability to do justice to a subject with which only the genius of a Scott or of a Burns could competently engage.

The Author craves, therefore, the kind indulgence of the courteous reader in his perusal of these pages; and, should he consider they lack that interest, he is requested to visit the district which they attempt to describe, and he will find attraction without limit, of the most interesting and imposing character.

PORT OF MONTEITH STATION,
June 1, 1867.

CONTENTS.

SUMMER

AT THE

LAKE OF MONTEITH.

INCHMAHOME.

INCHMAHOME, the subject of the present volume, is a beautiful little island, of about five acres in extent, situated near the centre of the Lake of Monteith, beautifully adorned with trees, and contains the ruins of one of the most ancient priories in Scotland. The Lake of Monteith is a beautiful sheet of water, near the south-western extremity of Perthshire. Situated in one of Scotland's fairest vales, and adorned with three isolated islands, this charming lake becomes at once an object of placid beauty, surrounded by a touch of real grandeur. On the north, tower the heath-clad hills of Monteith, the home of the wild cat and the eagle—the abode of the wolf and wild boar of old—the hiding-place of the outlaw and war-chief of other days. Here the kilted warrior met his steel-clad foe; for,

> " Of later fields of feud and fight,
> When, pouring from their Highland height,
> The Scottish clans, in headlong sway,
> Had swept the scarlet ranks away;"

when the fern-covered rocks re-echoed with all the thun-

B

ders of war—sounds long since chased away by the music
of the herdsman's pipe, or the song of the shepherd's
daughter. On the west, are the rugged passes and scattered crags of Aberfoyle, with the heath-capped hills of
the country of Rob Roy. On the south, are the dark
forests of Cardross, where the roe roams free and the
ospray rears her young; and on the east, mansions dot its
pebbled shores, with the lone country highway winding
along the sandy beach, like a huge native adder in its
coils, cooling its poisoned tongue in the silvery waters.
Landing on Inchmahome, one hundred feet from the shore
the Priory looms before you in gloomy grandeur, the
melancholy wreck of its former glory—hoary, holy pile,
gray with age, crumbling to decay before Time's withering
hand, but still a monument of the zeal and industry of its
early founders!

The eastern gable of the Priory is thirty feet wide and
three storeys high, and is supported by strong buttresses.
There is one beautiful window in this portion of the
building. It looks towards the lake, and the arches, five
in number, are still standing.

The north wall is one hundred feet long, from the
eastern gable to what is called the "Bell Tower," and
twenty-one feet again from the corner of the tower to
the western gable. This wall has four windows; these
however, are of plain workmanship. The north door,
situated near the centre of the building, is also of plain
work. The holy water basin stood at the north corner
of the entrance-hall, leading up towards the grand altar;
and from this point there seems to have been a direct

communication with the Nunnery, situated on a more southern portion of the Island, and it appears to have been arched over, as part of the arches still remain. The holy water basin was a beautiful relict of the past, and might long have remained to point the mind back to the days that are gone, had not an ignorant native taken it into his head that money was concealed below it, and smashed it to pieces. The marks of this murderous pick are still visible. This basin was hewn out of solid stone, beautifully ornamented; and, until recently destroyed, was as perfect as when it left the chisel, seven hundred years ago.

Between the corner, where stand the remains of the basin, and the "Bell Tower," there had originally been four arched gateways, complete trophies of the exquisite chisel of the mason of old. Two of these alone now remain, but are sufficient to convince us of their beautiful and delicate workmanship. An image, in a most entire state, stands on a broken arch near to the tower, and is said to represent St. Colmicus. This stone was found a few years ago, imbedded among the ruins, and placed in its present position by the proprietor.

The Bell Tower appears to have been of later construction than the Priory, as one of the aforementioned arches is completely covered by it, the tower having been built in its direct front. This building is twelve feet square inside, and is four storeys high. The top was reached by a winding stair; and, from the "Bellman's window," a fine view of lake and mountain scenery could be had. The lower portion was used by the last Earls as a dungeon.

The western gable is thirty feet wide; and the principal
object of attraction is the main gateway, a perfect triumph
of Gothic architecture, which displays, in a wonderful degree, the perfection of ancient masonic art. There is here
an exhibition of masonic skill rarely to be met with, even
in old monastic buildings. Being much exposed to the
weather, however, the fine grooving and minute chisel work
are slowly but surely crumbling away. The wall over the
archway has been adorned with five images, but the ra-
vages of time have very nearly defaced them. One or
two of these are entirely worn off, but on the remain-
der, the faint outlines of a face can yet be traced. The
doorway is twelve feet high and six feet wide; and, in
our boyish days, some large trees had their roots on the
ruined wall immediately above, and spread their gray
antlers wide to the breeze, but these have been cut down
to preserve the building. One large root still, like a
mighty serpent, creeps among the aged stones, and hides
its head in waving ferns.

A considerable portion of the south wall has succumbed
to time, and has fallen down several feet. This is much
to be regretted; as it gives a sort of ragged appearance
to the otherwise entire building. There have been four
arched windows in this portion of the building. Two
of these, however, have been thrown down, but the re-
maining two prove that they were moulded by the same
cunning hand that adorned other parts of this ancient
edifice.

The choir of the church has long been used as a burying-
ground, probably for five or six hundred years; and here

repose the dust of earls and chiefs of clans, and men who, in days long gone by, had measured lances on the hillside, when clan met clan in deadly feud. We enter the " lonely biggin'," and, as the massive gate reels back on its hinges, ravens croak and owls flap their wings. Hush, ye tenants of the air! ye disturb the slumbers of the " mighty dead." We step lightly, for we are treading on the dust of heroes of other days. It requires no marble slab on the ruined wall to tell of your ancient glory: the dark and misty track of five hundred years has failed to efface it—the memory of the Stewart, the Drummond, and De Græme can never perish! Here, below each moss-covered stone, are men of fame and graves of historic renown. Before us, in " sculptured stone," arm in arm with his Countess, rests the hero of Largs; on our left, are the graves of the Grahams of Gartur, Phaedal, Rednock, Leechtown, and Soyock; on our right, the Grahams of Gartmore, Glenny, Mondhuie; and, close to the north wall, sleep the founders of the ducal house of Drummond, the descendants of the Hanoverian King. And here too (but, dear reader, only whisper it!) rest the ashes of Sir John Menteith, the betrayer of Wallace; but all trace of his grave has been lost—in fact, wilfully forgotten.

A few yards south of the Priory stands the burying-vault of the last Earls of Menteith and Airth. This has been a two-storey building, with arched vaults, the latter being seated round with hewn stone. There are two very entire windows in this building, the one of three arches, the other of two. The entrance to the vault was by a grand arched hall, one hundred feet long, and led in from the

west. On each side of the gateway stood the crests of the
Earls of Menteith and Airth.

Adjoining the aforementioned vault, and on the south
side, stand the ruins of a large nunnery,* said to be the
oldest building on the island. It measures nearly one
hundred feet long, and the lower storey has been arched
over. One of the apartments, the kitchen, is still standing
—the large chimney and fireplace being very entire. The
windings of a stair which has reached to some high portion
of the building can also be traced.

On the south-western portion of the island, and surrounded by a broken-down wall, is the original flower
garden of the Earls of Menteith. This plot of ground is
thirty-five yards square, and in the centre stands a fine
old boxwood tree, said to have been planted by Queen
Mary. Notwithstanding its having weathered the storm
of ages, it is in a fine healthy and growing state. This
tree measures upwards of three feet in circumference, and
has beautifully spread branches.

On a gentle rising knoll, at the western side of the
aforementioned flower-plot, stands what is called "Queen
Mary's Bower," said to have been planted by her own
tiny hand; and such a spot could only be chosen by a
Queen. This most interesting little spot measures thirty-
three yards round the outside, and was originally adorned
with a row of boxwood trees, planted at regular intervals,
with a thorn in the centre; but through neglect, the plun-

---

* This building is traditionally called "The Nunnery," but for what reason I
cannot discover, there being no note in history that there had ever been a nunnery
or nuns on the island. Graham of Duchray says it was the "dwellings of the
churchmen."

dering of tourists, and the blasts of three hundred years, only five of those hallowed relics of the past wave their green heads over the ancient playground of the Royal Maiden. Several years ago, the thorn succumbed to the gale, but happily a tender shoot sprung from the torn roots, and now stands, like a young queen, on the place where its parent stood of old. A neat modern railing now secures this sacred spot from profane hands, and a row of young boxwood from the parent stems grows green around it. We linger long near this ancient bower, the only living emblem of a long unhappy past; for our fancy delights to roam amid such scenes, and wander back to the time

> When monarchs, far from din of court,
> Did to thy fairy shades resort;
> And maiden queens, with joyous smile,
> Sported through the sylvan isle.

A gentle eminence, on the south-eastern corner of the island, bears the name of the "Nun's Hill;"* and on this knoll, it is said, the nuns used to disport themselves, and gather peebles on the shore, during the intervals of their holy functions. A communication from the Nunnery—by a walk, guarded on each side by high walls,

---

* Universal tradition sets this knoll down as the "Nun's Hill," and the tradition regarding it is a rather singular one. A nun, who having fallen in love with a son of one of the first Earls of Menteith, resolved to throw aside the veil, break her vow, and leave the dungeons of Cambuskenneth for the sweets of Talla. A meeting had been arranged on this particular spot, and a boat provided on the eastern shore to take the nun to Inchmahome. But, alas for love! a neighbouring clan invaded the Earl's domain, and leading his father's clansmen against the foe, the brave youth fell on the dark braes of Mondhuie. In his last moments, the youth unconsciously divulged to his confessor his meeting with the nun. Enraged at the insult offered to his church, the cruel monk resolved to be revenged. Disguised as the young nobleman, he watched the arrival of the runaway nun. Well, 'twas a

and still called the "Nun's Walk"—led to this place of retirement, and completely screened them from the vulgar gaze. This mound appears to have been partly natural and partly artificial. It has finely sloping sides, with flat top, and a large oak tree spreads its withered arms around its summit; while, at the east side, a beautiful specimen of native fir hangs its green tresses over the ancient walk, once trod by holy feet alone.

Between a point on the south side of the island and the adjacent "Talla" or "Earl's Isle," there is an echo that will repeat several words at a time; and oft has this "hollow sound" returned the holy voice of a monk or nun, and sent back the thundering tones of a belted knight or warrior, or whispered from isle to isle the lisping accents of the virgin Queen, as the fairy thing sported along the pebbled shore.

The Island of Inchmahome is beautifully wooded; many of the trees have attained an immense size, and have spread their antlered heads for ages over its hallowed soil. A number of these monarchs of the forest have yielded to the gale, and their gigantic trunks lie scattered over the soil that gave them birth, telling the spectator

clear moonlight night when the monk threw aside the gown and cowl for a warrior's dress, and took his place on the appointed spot. By-and-by a small black speck is seen on the Inchie shore; 'twas the nun in her lover's boat. She, footsore and weary, had trod the plain from Stirling to the lake, and was now pushing her scallop over the tiny waves. Shortly the boat touched the sand, and the fair lady sprang into her supposed lover's arms; but, alas! it was only to be hurled back to perish in the blue waters. Next day the monks on the island had the body taken from the lake, and interred in an upright posture on the knoll—hence the "Nun's Hill." A large stone near the top of the hill marks the supposed spot. At a certain hour in the evening, tradition says, a dark figure may yet be seen treading the "Nun's Hill."

that the most noble of earth's productions will eventually pass away. The western half of the island united with "Talla," the Earl's residence, to form the Earl's demesne; and, but a few years ago, Inchmahome could boast of a rare and beautiful orchard, but which has unfortunately been allowed to fall into decay. The tourist no longer looks upon the trees beneath whose boughs earls roamed, or monarchal hands plucked the golden fruit. Brighter days, however, are dawning on the "Isle of rest;" and we trust that the good work of restoration already begun will go on until every breach be repaired, and the rubbish, that lies scattered like wreck after a debauch, be swept away.

There is much in Inchmahome for the instruction of the tourist, the study of the geologist, and the admiration of the antiquarian. As a place of beauty and retirement— where Nature has richly displayed her varied charms— combined with the ever hallowed associations that are heard in every echo, that linger in every glen, that rest on the heathery hillside, and are wafted back by every balmy breeze which floats around its shores — the Lake of Monteith, and the fairy islands that nestle on its bosom, stand alone in their glory.

The era of monasteries is a date long gone by, "far off and dim," a story of an early age; and it is only when we look back along the dark and misty track of history, that we ever and anon get a glimpse of the time when those "oases in the natural and moral wilderness" reared their heads throughout the dark corners of our land. We must note the era of these as the dawn of civilisation among a warlike and savage people, and in those dark ages they

must have spread a healthful influence around them. The
monks tilled the soil, and the peasants followed their example. At early dawn and dewy eve they chanted the
praises of God; and warriors, attired only in their kilts,
with naked swords, bowed their heads to listen. By their
example, industry was promoted, and holy religion spread
throughout the land. But, alas! time changed with the
roll of centuries, and, through the gifts of the great and
the good, monasteries swelled into magnificence. Instead
of "growing in grace," however, they became the abodes
of revelry, riot, and dissipation; their glory faded; and
the day arrived when they had to be swept from the earth
as an abomination, and only left behind them those noble
wrecks—standing stark, like gigantic skeletons—the wonder
and admiration of later years.

The Monastery of Inchmahome is the very earliest
Augustinian monastery in Scotland, and was an extensive
and noted one, the existing ruins bearing proof of its once
ancient grandeur. The Priory was founded by Edgar,
King of Scotland, who succeeded to the throne on the
death of his father, Malcolm III., in the year 1098. The
Priory belonged to the Canons regular of the Augustinian
order; it was originally connected with the Abbey of
Cambuskenneth, and had four dependent chapels. It
does not appear that Edgar did more than establish
religious men on the island during his reign, for it is
certain that the church at least was either erected or
rebuilt by Walter Cumyn, Lord of Badenoch, who married
the eldest daughter of the Earl of Menteith. And from
the document authorising Cumyn to build a religious

house on the island, it appears that it was originally in
the diocese of Dunblane; for, says that paper, " the said
Bishop of Dunblane, in the name of his church, for himself and all his successors, shall renounce all right which
the said bishops or their predecessors, in the name of
the church of Dunblane, have, had, or might or could
have, in lands, or money-rents received from lands, and
in all revenues and rents annually drawn in name of pen-
sions from the church of the Earldom of Menteith."

Inchmahome was united by James IV. to the Chapel
Royal of Stirling, but was afterwards dissolved from the
College, and bestowed by James V. on John Erskine, third
son of Lord Erskine. Erskine having outlived his brothers,
succeeded his father as Lord Erskine. He afterwards ac-
quired the title of Earl of Mar, and was elected Regent of
Scotland. It appears from an Act in the reign of James
VI., that Cardross, in Monteith, belonged to the Priory;
for, according to said Act, entituled " Act of annexation of
Forfaulted Landis and Rentis to the Crown," the lands of
Cardross are therein described as " feu lands of Inchmahome."

That Inchmahome had long been an occasional royal
residence is fully authenticated by history. We find from
Buchanan that Duncan II., King of Scotland, was murdered
here in the year 1094, by M'Pender, the Earl of Mearns.
M'Pender was bribed by Donald Bane, the deposed monarch, to assassinate his king, and being a factious nobleman,
marched to Monteith, under the cloud of night, and succeeded in killing Duncan and afterwards making his escape.
Tradition asserts that King Edgar, who reigned from the

year 1098 to 1107, resided frequently on the island. There is, however, no other historical notice of royalty having been on the island till Bruce's visit on the 15th of April 1310, and it was then the scene of his issuing some royal prerogatives. One of these is the confiscating of all the goods, movable and immovable, of John de Pollox, who is described as an enemy of the King; and concludes, "Given at the island of Saint Colmicus, the fifteenth day of April, in the year of grace one thousand three hundred and ten, and fifth year of our reign." Queen Mary was carried to Inchmahome by her guardian, the Marquis of Montrose, and Lord Erskine, immediately after the battle of Pinkie, in September 1543.* It is not correctly known how long Mary resided here, but there is a space of three months from the date of Pinkie to the time when she sailed from Dumbarton for France, and it is generally believed that the most of that time was spent on Inchmahome, where she planted the boxwood bower that still retains the name of its royal founder.

James VI. is said to have been the last crowned head that sought the sweets of retirement in Inchmahome, and this is supposed to have been when the King was on a visit to his old class-fellow, the Earl of Mar, at Cardross House.

Among the many royal sports practised on the Island of Inchmahome, none is said to have been so popular with the "crowned heads" as that of fishing with geese. This singular and original mode gave much amusement to the spectators, and was of a most interesting kind. A number of geese were let loose upon the lake, each having a line

---

* Some writers say three months, others two years.

with hook and bait attached to its leg. The poor goose
would not proceed far before some huge pike would pounce
upon the bait, and then began "the tug of war." As soon
as the fish found itself hooked, it would dart far amid the
blue waters, dragging the unwary goose below the surface;
but, instantly recovering itself, the· noble fowl would flap
his wings and make the vain endeavour to fly off,' but
would be again and again drawn back. By-and-by, however, the distinguished member of the farm-yard would
prove too much for his adversary, and the floundering pike
would be landed in triumph.

Interesting as every spot on the Island of Inchmahome
is—its ruined walls, its "sky-roofed halls," the King's
walks, and the Queen's garden,—yet there is none so full
of deep interest, and that tends to carry the mind back to
the dark vista of time when the mantle of oppression hung
its thick and sable folds deep around Scotland, than the
last resting-place of the heroes of other days. Side by
side sleep those early champions—warriors who had robed
themselves in martial glory in their country's cause; and
though many of them live but .in tradition, and on the
stones that cover them, their memory will for ever find a
place in the bosom of an ever-grateful native population.

The first grave that attracts attention, is one immediately
in front of the entrance-gate, consisting of two figures in
sculptured stone, executed in bas-relief, representing Walter Stewart and his Countess. This Walter Stewart was
son of Alexander, the High Steward of Scotland. He
married the' second daughter of the Earl of Menteith, and
succeeded to the Earldom on the death of Cumyn, who

was married to the eldest daughter. The historian of the
house of Buchanan asserts that he was married to the
heiress of Cumyn. This Walter Stewart was a very prominent man of his time, and took part in all the leading
incidents of the day. He commanded a part of the army
at the battle of Largs, when Haco, King of Norway, invaded Scotland, in 1293. He was a distinguished Crusader
under Louis IX. of France; and was one of the arbiters
on the part of Bruce, in his competition for the crown
with John Baliol. Walter had two sons, Murdoch, his
successor, and Sir John Menteith of Rusky, the betrayer
of Sir William Wallace, and the ancestor of all those of
the surname of Menteith. There is here, perhaps, the
greatest contrast between a father and son to be found in
the history of this or any other country. The father, it
would seem, during the whole tenor of his days, had but
one grand object next his heart—the welfare of his heart-
broken, bleeding country; and the strength of his interest
and the prowess of his arm were used in securing for
Scotland her lawful rights, and ridding her shores of foreign
oppressors ;—the son selling, for a paltry reward, the
greatest hero that ever trod its soil!

The next spot that attracts attention, is the last resting-
place of the illustrious members of the house of Drummond
—the tombstone being of the most ancient and interesting kind. This remarkable stone is executed in bas-
relief, and the carving represents the figure of a knight
in full armour, accompanied by the archangel Michael,
and St. Colmicus trampling on the dragon. The inscription is much wasted by its great age; and, by the gross

carelessness of those in charge of the island some years ago, the stone unfortunately got broken. It reads thus: —"John of Drumod, son of Malcolm of Drumod. His widow, that she may loose their souls from punishment and the sting." The intelligent reader will understand that "Drumod" is the ancient Celtic pronunciation of Drummond. This stone is proof that the Priory was dedicated to St. Michael; and St. Michael's fair used to be held on the farm of Miling, on the shores of the lake. Sir John Drummond, represented on this stone, was son-in-law of Walter Stewart, Earl of Menteith, and brother-in-law to Sir John, the betrayer. Sir John succeeded his father about the year 1278. He was said to have been a man " of great parts and influence." He was the eighth chief of his family, and Thane or Earl of Lennox. At the hot discussions and violent contests that raged in Scotland about the succession of Alexander III., he took a prominent part in Bruce's cause. His son Malcolm was a keen supporter of Robert Bruce, and distinguished for his opposition to the English king. Malcolm was, however, taken prisoner in the year 1301, by John Seagrave; and so great was the joy of the English monarch, that, on the 25th of October of the same year, he offered public thanks in the Cathedral of Glasgow for the "good news." Sir Malcolm was, on this occasion, compelled to swear fealty to Edward, and was afterwards set at liberty. On his return to Monteith, however, he renounced all allegiance to the English king, and repaired at once, with his vassals, to the standard of Bruce; and thus we find him once more face to face with his old enemy. He afterwards took a prominent part in the battle of Bannockburn, which resulted so disastrously to the English. Immediately after the battle, he was gifted with extensive grants of lands; and, being of a very pious turn of mind, he conferred upon the Priory of Inchmahome his estate of Cardross.

There was another true defender of his country, Sir John, son of the above Malcolm Drummond. This Sir John had a mortal hatred of his cousins, the Menteiths of Rusky, the grandsons of the betrayer. And it requires no great stretch of fancy to imagine how this would occur, seeing that the family of the Drummonds were warm adherents of their country, and the others its mortal and direst enemies. Whether it was to revenge his own private quarrel; or for the purpose of punishing the Menteith family for the disloyalty and the disgrace brought upon the country, we have no means of knowing, but history affords us a clue to the terrible results. The traditions of the country are, however, that it was a bold and determined plan, on the part of Drummond, to destroy, at once and for ever, every seed of the obnoxious family. Accordingly, early in the year 1360, he attacked the Menteiths near Rusky with a strong band of his chosen vassals. The Menteiths collected in great force to defend themselves, but were unable to cope with the fierce character of Drummond, and they received at his hand a terrible chastisement, three out of five brothers of the Menteiths being slain, besides a great number of their followers. Some short time after this deadly fray, an agreement was effected between the families, and Sir John Drummond renounced to the youngest of the two surviving brothers of the Menteiths, as compensation for the slaughter, the estate of Roseneath. The treaty between the chiefs of the two families is dated "Banks of the Forth, near Strivelyn, 17th May 1360." Sir John was married to the heiress of Montifex, and their only daughter was the accomplished Queen of Robert III., and said to have been born at Drumnacaistal, near Drymen, and for which the people of Drymen ought to feel justly proud.

"The Story of the Drummonds," as it is called in tradition, is a curious and singular one, and had a very important bearing on the early history of Scotland.

During the reign of Malcolm III. of Scotland, there was staying at the Court of the King of England a young foreign prince, the son of the King of Hungary. He was pious, young, and brave, and was a great favourite at Court. The King, too, had an only daughter, the affianced bride of the King of Scotland; and when the time drew near when she was to leave her home and her fatherland, to become the Queen of the northern monarch, Maurice, "the young Hun," as he was called, being soldier and sailor as well, was selected chief of the staff that was to escort the fair maiden to her distant home. With tears in his eyes, and his heart at the breaking, the old monarch handed his young daughter over to the charge of the prince, and he sailed away from England's shore. When the maiden's heart grew weary, and longed for her father's Court, he cheered her up with hope, told her stories of love, and sung the war hymns of his native land. All went well, and at last the shores of old Scotia dawned in view. It was the last night at sea; the sun sank behind the still

c

waters with unusual splendour; and all but one spoke of
a happy landing on the shores of their new home.   There
was one old sailor there who shook his head, stroked his
grey beard, and whispered doubts of the morrow, as he
scanned the western sky.   During the night all was still;
but in early morn the stillness awoke into a breeze, the
breeze broke into a storm, and with daylight came the
hurricane, and all around was tempest and roaring sea.
The wild waves rolled, the wind howled, and the sails
flapped; while the frail bark creaked from stem to stern,
and drifted fast ashore.

Hope fled from every breast.   Behind was the raging
sea; before, the rugged rocks; around was heard the cries
of drowning sailors, the crash of falling masts, and the
din of floating timber.   Calm and unruffled stood the
young Hun, with a tender maiden half dead in his
arms.   One wave rolled past; and he gazed at it, but
hesitated.   Another, greater than the first, came rolling on;
but still he only looked on its foaming surface.   Another,
greater than the two, came hissing after; and, lifting his
heart to Him who had brought him safe from fiery foe and
battle-field, he sprang amid the angry tide and was rolled
ashore, and, with the grasp of despair, clutching the
rock, and dragging himself and the unconscious maid up
on to the crags, he landed England's Princess and Scotland's Queen safe on land.

He took the three waves for his coat of arms, and for his
bravery he received from the Scotch King extensive grants
of lands.   So says tradition; history tells the rest.   He was
gifted by King Malcolm with the lands of Drummond, and

was afterwards known as Maurice De Drummond.* All the early chiefs of the house of Drummond are interred in the choir of Inchmahome. There is another remarkable grave-stone in the choir, it is also executed in bas-relief, and bears the arms of the Grahams, with the following initials carved upon it, " G. D. E. D." being the initial letters of the words " *Gloria Deo Esto Data;*" " Let glory be inscribed to God." This stone is also of antiquity, and appears to have been the burying-place of the first Earls of the name of Graham.

* He had also Cardross, Balfron, and Roseneath ,

TRADITIONS REGARDING SIR JOHN MENTEITH.

SIR JOHN MENTEITH was the second son of Walter Stewart, Earl of Menteith, and was born on the island of Inchmahome. On the death of his father, Sir John succeeded to the estate of Rusky, and resided

> " Where the majestic Grampians spread
>   Their shadow o'er old Rusky's head;
> Where friendship warms the escutcheoned walls
>   Of frowning Rusky's antique halls."

Sir John selected as his place of residence a small island on Loch Rusky—a dark and deep, but beautiful sheet of water, about midway between Callander and Lake of Monteith, having a commanding view of the surrounding country. On this little island he built a strong castle, the ruins of which still remain. Sir John is reported to have kept a fleet stud of horses, for the purpose of carrying out his traitorous designs with the English king; and, in support of this tradition, the course for training the horses is still to be seen on the banks of the loch. Another of Sir John's castles was the Castle of Monteith, now called Castle of Rednock, a considerable portion of which is still standing. This castle was originally very strong, of great dimensions, and beautifully situated beneath a proud wing of the Grampians, from the summit of which there is one of the most varied and commanding views in Scotland. One roll of the traitor's eye could view the country from Leith to

Lennox—that fertile country, studded with trees, dotted with villages, and rivers rolling through its plains—the very garden of Scotland—the cradle of Scottish patriots. When occasion served, Scotland's direst enemy—he who was nurtured in her own arms, and who spilt her best blood— swept from his impregnable fortress, like the wild eagle from his eyrie, upon his doomed prey. Many reasons are assigned as the cause of Menteith betraying Wallace. Some assert that he was dissatisfied with the conduct of Wallace on some particular occasion. Supposing this to be true, it is no justification why he should deceive his early friend; for, according to Barbour, Sir John was one of Wallace's earliest friends. For my own part, I am ready to believe that it is only a glaring proof of the deceitfulness of the human heart, prompted by English gold, which had unfortunately found its way to the shores of the Lake of Monteith. The attempt of Sir John to betray Bruce in Dumbarton Castle is another proof that the man was a base-hearted villain. There is an attempt made by one historian to whitewash Sir John of the crime of betraying Wallace. It is, however, but a miserable " daub," and not borne out by a single writer except himself; and alluding to the betrayal, other writers declare that he was justly and deservedly hated by the Scotch nation. The manner of the betrayal is well known; how, when they met at Robroyston, the two chiefs recognised each other as old familiar friends; and how Menteith had previously arranged with Edward's spies about the turning of the " loaf" when the favourable moment arrived for falling on and securing the chief of Scottish patriots. It was for a very long time

asserted, that the deepest insult one could give to an individual of the name of Menteith was the turning of the loaf
in his presence, thus calling to mind that they were the
descendants of the infamous Sir John. I have known,
even in my own day, a fiery Menteith take signal vengeance on a fellow-mortal who had the audacity to "whum-
mel the bannock" in his presence.

The tradition regarding the attempt of Menteith to betray Bruce is not generally known. The story, however,
varies a good deal, and is told in different forms; but as
Buchanan alludes to it, and as his version will no doubt
be the most correct, I have followed that historian pretty
closely. When the rest of the fortified places were reduced,
Dumbarton Castle was held almost alone by the English;
and because it was by nature very strong, Bruce entered
into negotiation with Menteith, who had received the go-
vernorship as the price of Wallace, through his friends
and relations, for its recovery. As the price of the surrender, Menteith had the "cheek" to demand the Earldom
of Lennox, and would listen to no other proposal. Bruce
would listen to no such condition, although he greatly desired the Castle—Lennox being his firmest and almost only
friend in all his misfortunes. The Earl himself, as soon
as he heard this, insisted that the King should not refuse
the condition. The agreement was therefore completed on
Menteith's own terms, and the King went to receive possession of the Castle. On his journey, he was met in the
wood near Dumbarton by a joiner, said to be named Rol-
land, who, having obtained an audience of the King on a
matter of great importance, discovered to him a plot, pro-

jected and prepared by Menteith against him. In an underground cellar a considerable number of Englishmen were hid, who, when the rest of the Castle was given up, and the King seated at dinner, were to rush forth and either kill or take him prisoner. After Bruce had received the Castle from Menteith, he was invited to an entertainment. The King, however, refused to partake until he had searched the concealed cellars. Menteith pretended that the smith who had the key was absent and would soon return, but the door was broken open and the snare discovered. The armed English were instantly put to death; some having confessed that a war-ship was riding in the bay, ready to convey the King to England. Sir John's life was spared, on condition that he should be put in the very front of the battle at Bannockburn, and take "pot luck." There, it is said, he served his King faithfully. I have not been able to trace where Sir John died, or where he was buried, though tradition asserts he died in his castle on Loch Rusky, and was interred in the choir of the church of Inchmahome.

TRADITION REGARDING THE DECLINE OF THE EARLDOM.

CONNECTED with the Earldom were some of the bravest warriors and most accomplished statesmen of the ages in which it flourished; and at Court the holders of the title took precedence over most other sister titles, while many of the Earls enjoyed, in a remarkable degree, the confidence of their Sovereign. But "every dog has its day;" and although we can trace the history of those feudal lords over a period of five hundred years, and that during a time when Scotland was boiling with internal divisions, yet the day arrived when the Earldom passed away and was known no more. Among the first Earls of note was Murdacus, who held the title about the year 1260. He had two daughters; the eldest was married to Cumin, Lord of Badenoch, who succeeded to the Earldom by right of his wife. Cumin was succeeded in the Earldom by Walter Stewart, brother of the High Steward of Scotland; who was married to the youngest daughter. Walter had two sons, Murdoch, his successor, and John Menteith of Rusky. Murdoch the Earl had one son, Allan, who married the heiress of Macduff, Earl of Fife. Allan had one daughter, married to Patrick Graham of Kilbride, second son of Patrick Graham of Kincardine. This Patrick Graham was the founder of the Earls of Menteith of the name of Graham, and whose posterity were Earls thereof for nine successive generations.

The Earldom became extinct in the year 1694. The last Earl, William, dying without issue, bequeathed his estates to the family of Montrose. The first cadet of the Menteith family was Sir John Graham of Kilbride, ancestor of the Grahams of Gartmore; and the last of any note was the ancestor of the Grahams of Gartur.

Local tradition assigns the decline of the Earldom to the cruelty of its last possessor, and among current stories the undernoted is believed to be the most authentic, while it illustrates, in a remarkable degree, the character of the times. A man of the name of Graham having stolen a horse in the neighbourhood, exposed the animal for sale at St. Michael's fair, then held on Miling farm, on the shores of the lake. Some of Graham's friends being present at the fair, told him the owner of the horse was on his track, and advised the thief instantly to leave the market. Graham, acting on the advice, asked a young lad of the name of Blair, who was standing by, to hold his horse till he transacted some trivial business, and immediately took to the hills. Meantime the owner of the horse arrived, and finding the unsuspecting Blair in possession, had him handed over to the tender mercies of the Earl, who was present at the fair; and in those "good old times" the Earl, who had the power of life and death in his own hands, the executioners in his own household, and the gallows on his own domains, ordered the lad to be instantly hanged. The Blairs at this time were a numerous party, both in Monteith and Aberfoyle, and many of the lad's friends being present at the fair, they made a strong remonstrance, but in vain. The sentence was instantly carried into effect on the Gal-

lows hill, a small eminence on the farm of Miling. The
Blairs were so enraged that they mustered in strong force,
and tore down the gallows, declaring that it should never
"hing" another man in Monteith; while an old woman
prophesied the downfal of the Earldom. She is said to
have told the Earl to his face that he would be the last of
his race, and that no other Graham should ever enjoy the
title; that his estate would pass away to the stranger; that
briars and thistles would grow rank in his rooms—the otter
make his home in the broken walls—and the jackdaw and
the owl build their nests amid the ruins. What effect this
imprecation had on the decline of the Earldom, I leave the
reader to judge; but the writer has had proof enough that
the latter part of it has been fulfilled with a vengeance.
Briars and thistles certainly grow rank around the crumbling walls, and the otter roams free amid their dark recesses;
while the jackdaw and the owl flap their wings at pleasure
in the once lordly halls of Talla.

TRADITIONAL BATTLES.

It was morning, and the eastern sun had thrown his first golden rays over the scattered crags of the heath-clad hills of Monteith, whose shaggy sides sent their dark shadows deep into the lake, whose waters reflected back the glories of the blue-vaulted heaven. All was peace in the walls of Talla. Zephyrs played around its shores, and the finny tribe sported on the surface of the peaceful waters; the fox sought the thick copse of Glenny, and the ospray floated over the lake. There was no sound to disturb the lonely sentinel, save the quack of the wild drake, or the plunge of the otter, as it dashed through the blue water after its finny prey. Suddenly, dashing through the copsewood, there appeared on the distant shore the picturesque form of a Highlander. Sword in hand, and dressed only in his kilt, the youth, without waiting for a boat, plunged amid the silvery breakers, and was soon within the tower of Talla, telling his chief that the Murrays of Atholl were plundering the glen. Instantly the war-cry sped along the valley, and soon

> The fiery cross proclaimed,
> And bugle sounded far—
> Rise up, ye kindred of the Græme!
> Follow thy chief to war.

Soon the whole followers of the Græme in the vale of Monteith were assembled to repel the northern invader,

headed by a younger son of the Earl, who addressed them
thus:—

> " Men of Monteith! yonder's the foemen!
> Bare your claymore and follow the bowmen.
> See yonder dark host up by yon rill—
> The Murrays of Atholl who cover the hill!
> They've come from the north to feed on thy spoil,
> And see how proudly they tread on thy soil.
> But now you will meet them, and drive them afar—
> For the kindred of Græme are gallant in war;
> The life of Blair-Atholl ye'll spill like a flood,
> Till the eagles of Glenny be drunk on the blood.
> On to the fray! and stay only when
> The corpses of Atholl lie thick in the glen;
> For the Græme he will conquer or die on the heath,
> That glory may dwell on the Lake of Monteith!"

So saying, onward rushed the eager youth up the tangled
slopes of his native Mondhuie, and over the rocks that had
oft rung with his hunting horn, and re-echoed back the war-
cry of his fathers. Græme was surrounded by his hardy
clansmen, all eager to meet the " men of the north," who
were hurrying down the hill-side,

> " Plaided and plumed in their tartan array "

As soon as the Murrays saw the approaching Grahams, it
is said they looked upon them with a sort of disdain, as
birds of inferior plumage—as the eagle looks down upon
the tenants of nether air,—and their chief exclaimed,
" Take the eagle's feathers off your arrows and put on
the goose's feathers; that's good enough for the Monteith
fellows." Ha! ha!—

> " Proud bird of the mountain! thy plume shall be torn."

A very severe hand-to-hand contest ensued, and many
fell on both sides. The Grahams, led by their young
chief, were pursuing their enemies over the hill, when a

wounded Atholl man, standing behind a tree, saw the leader of the Grahams approach the spot where he was concealed, drew his dagger, and, as Græme was hurrying past, plunged it into his side. The Grahams were so exasperated at this act, that the perpetrator was instantly despatched, and his friends driven off with great loss. The Grahams had their wounded chief carried from the hill, and Talla opened her halls to receive her bleeding lord. With his last breath he sung—

> " The blood of the slain is tinging yon rill,
> For the dead thick are lying;
> But in peace I am dying,
> For the Murrays are flying
> Far over the hill."

There is another version of this battle, as follows:— The chief of the Atholl men, being on friendly terms with the Earl, called at the island to pay him a friendly visit. Unfortunately, however, the Earl chanced to be out hunting, and the Atholl men finding the boats on the north side of the lake, a number of the party sailed over to the island, where they found a well-cooked dinner, consisting of a large number of finely dressed fowls, &c., all laid out, waiting the Earl's return. The Murrays swept the hall of everything eatable, and took their departure. The Earl soon returned, and found that his roasted fowls had taken wing, with the exception of an old cock, which had "craw'd" the clan to arms for ten years; and, on being told by the cook what had taken place, he instantly ordered his retainers to pursue the fugitives, and led the pursuit in person. Coming up with the Atholl men on the hill of Mondhuie, he was about to fall on them and revenge the insult, when the leader of the pursued turned round, and, presenting his arrow, cried, in a friendly tone, "Over me and over you!" —meaning, that each should shoot his arrow over his opponent's head, and thus end the matter without loss of life. "Na, na," exclaimed the insulted chief, "in me and in you." "In you be it then!" thundered Murray; and, instantly raising his arrow, shot the Earl through the heart.

This fray gained for this branch of the Grahams the appellation of the "Hen Grahams." A member of this branch quarrelled with a M'Gregor on the hill overlooking the lake. M'Gregor being angry, was about to call out "Hen Graham!" perceiving his intention, Graham instantly drew his sword and severed his head from his body. It is said that the head rolled to the foot of the hill calling out "Hen Graham, hen Graham!"

Another battle was fought on the shores of the Lake of Monteith, in the year 1653, between the Highlanders on one side, and a detachment of Cromwell's army on the other. The Highlanders consisted of men of the following clans, viz., Grahams, M'Gregors, M'Naughtons, and a number of horsemen under Lord Kenmure, all stationed at Duchray Castle, and under the command of Graham, Laird of Duchray, and the Earl of Glencairn, numbering in all about three hundred.

Colonel Kidd, then governor of Stirling Castle, being apprised of the meeting of the Royalists in Aberfoyle, marched at the head of a regiment of foot and a troop of horse, with a view to crush Duchray and his hardy little band, and, if possible, annihilate the enterprise. Graham of Glenny, hearing of the advance of Kidd, hastily collected his men, and hid them in ambush in the pass on the front of the hill overlooking the lake. Graham, having but a mere handful of men, was unable to take the advantage his position offered, but kept up a galling fire on the enemy. Among the Grahams was a young man, of the name of M'Queen, who was very conspicuous in emptying Kidd's saddles. Kidd, annoyed at the loss of his men, ordered his horsemen to dislodge the enemy. The horsemen instantly charged up the hill, and one of them singling out M'Queen, cut him down. The spot where he fell is still pointed out, and bears the name of " M'Queen's Pass." One of Kidd's horsemen singling out a Graham, galloped after him right up the steep pass and over the hill. Graham, running for his life, fled towards Portend Glen, a wild and rugged glen on the shores of the lake. As he approached the brink of the precipice, and the horseman was about to cut him down, Graham suddenly darted to one side, and in a moment afterwards the horse and his rider went thundering over the rocks. This part of the glen is still pointed out to tourists as " the Horseman's Rock." Glenny, on the first approach of Kidd, had sent notice to Duchray of the intended attack, and to prepare him for the enemy. Duchray, on learning this, instantly marched to meet him, and took up a strong position near the foot of Loch Ard, hiding his foot on the rising ground on each side of the road, and posting his horse in the centre. Presently Kidd arrived, and the unwary commander walked deliberately into the lion's embraces. At the word of command, the Highlanders sprang from their native heather,

" As if the yawning earth had given
A subterranean host to heaven;"

and, sweeping from the hill-sides like a mighty avalanche, overwhelmed his flanks, while the horsemen charging in front, threw the whole of the enemy into such wild confusion that it was impossible to rally them, and, fleeing in disorder, they became an easy prey to the broadswords of the High-landmen. One of Kidd's officers was shot by a private gentleman from the window of his house, which then stood near the foot of Loch Ard, and his body was interred in a little knoll, which still bears the name of "Badden Cass-nock," or "The Englishman's Thicket."

Regarding the early dilapidation of the Priory, I have been unable to gather the smallest information either from history or tradition. There is no doubt, however, that the Priory would share the fate of all other religious houses of the same kind at the period. We are told by Spottiswood "that no difference was made, but all the churches were either defaced or pulled down, and that the very sepulchres of the dead were not spared." The mischievous inclinations of the inhabitants, however, and the plundering raids of the modern natives, have done more towards the destruc-tion of the sacred edifice than the excited multitude of John Knox, or the roar of Cromwell's cannon.

The Priory of Inchmahome had four dependent chapels attached to it. One of these stood at the east side of the lake, on what is now part of the farm of Inchie, and a little to the north of where the Water of Goodie flows out of the lake. There is no part of the ruins visible, but a small point jutting out into the lake is still pointed out as the burying-ground attached to this religious house. Another was at Arnchly, that is "The Field of the Burying-ground," situated about a mile to the west of the lake. The ruins of the chapel and part of the burying-ground are still visible. Another was at the " Chapelaroch," that is, " The Foundation of the Chapel," about a mile below the village of Gartmore, and situated on the banks of the water of Kelty. The other was at Balquhapple, near Drymen. All these places, with the exception of Arnchly, still retain the name of Chapel.

There is a curious prophecy connected with a stone situated near the ruins of the chapel of Arnchly, and which is worth recording. From time immemorial this stone went under the name of the " Peace Stone," and it was held in great reverence by the natives. One Pharic M'Pharic, a noted Gaelic prophet, foretold that, in the course of time, this stone would be buried underground by two brothers, who, for their indiscretion, were to die childless. By-and-by the stone would rise to the surface, and by the time it was fairly above ground, a battle was to be fought on "Auchveity," that is, "Betty's Field." The battle was to be long and fierce, until "Gramoch-Cam" of Glenny, that is, "Graham of the one eye," would sweep from the "Bay-wood" with his clan and decide the contest. After the battle, a large raven was to alight on the stone and drink the blood of the fallen. So much for the prophecy then; now for the fulfilment. About fifty years ago, two brothers (tenants of the farm of Arnchly), finding that the stone interfered with their agricultural labours, made a large trench, and had it put several feet below the surface. Very singular, indeed, both these men, although married, died without leaving any issue. With the labouring of the field

D

for a number of years, the stone has actually made its appearance above ground, and there is at present living a descendant of the Grahams of Glenny. who is blind of one eye, and the ravens are daily hovering over the devoted field.   Tremble, ye natives! and rivals of the "Hero Grahams," keep an eye on Gramoch-Cam!

There is another very interesting tradition regarding "Betty's Field."   I leave the reader, however, to take it for what it may be worth.   In early times when Inchmahome was a royal residence, the country to the west of the lake was a royal forest, and the stag, the wolf, and the wild boar found a safe retreat amid its dark solitudes, when the glens rang with the hunter's horn, and re-echoed back the cry of royal sportsmen.   One morning the retainers of the King were summoned to join the royal chase, and to follow the train of his son, to hunt the stag.   On the border of the forest a stag was sighted, but instead of keeping on the high ground, it broke off towards the marsh, and was instantly followed by the Prince, who, heedless of the danger, kept thundering on till he reached the banks of a small but beautiful loch in the vicinity of Arnchly.   Here his horse got "bogged," and the royal rider was in imminent peril of his life.   A young "Hielan' lassie," however, chanced to be attending her cattle at the Sheals of Gartrench, a locality close by, and seeing the danger of her royal master, with great presence of mind rushed to his aid, and bore him off in her arms to a place of safety.   For her "distinguished services," the Prince was glad enough to be able to grant her for life the portion of land still called, and no doubt after her own name,

" Betty's Field." The little sequestered loch, on whose banks the incident occurred, is still called " Loch Mackin-veigh," that is, " The Loch of the King's son,"·which gives a colouring of truthfulness to the story. It is said that it was in this royal forest the last wolf seen in Scotland was killed, and that at a place called the " Claggans," on the farm of Miling.˙ It is also said that the same wolf attacked ɪ girl near the village of Gartmore, a short time previous to its death at Miling. The girl was carrying meat to the harvest people, when the animal rushed out of the " Fir hill." Being afraid, the girl threw the " beef and tatties" ɔn the ground and fled. The wolf was content with the dinner, and thus the girl escaped.

THE EARL'S NIECE.

"There's a ball in Talla to-night," said a Highland native to his companion, as they passed along the lone Highland highway that winds its serpentine form along the north shore of the Lake of Monteith, one clear moonlight night about the fall of the year. "Ay," returned the other, "I hear the music, and see how the lights flash in the windows!" They were right; there was a gathering of the chiefs within the lordly halls of Talla. The Chief of Buchan was there; Lord Rusky mingled with the guests; and Gartmore Barons strode through the hall; while the young Graham of Gloschoil, the Earl's kinsman, sat chatting with the Countess. The Earl was proud of his name, proud of his title, and jealous of his fame; his heart was the warm heart of the Highlander; his nature the fiery dash of the Celt—the first to resent an insult—the first to forgive an injury. When a friend or foe chanced to be injured, it grieved him at his heart, and could never be forgotten. The field was his delight. The halls of his fathers were hung with trophies of the chase. There were antlered heads from the forest of Miling, the wolf from Craigvad, and the wild boar from his den in the Pass; the eagle from Glenny, and the osprey from Arnmauch; the wild fox and badger from the hill, and the otter from the lake. There, too, dangled in gloomy array the glories of the war chief, wrecks of the battle-field, gathered by a long list of illustrious ancestors, each proud of his achievements, and whose trophies hung as heirlooms in the family. Largs sent its shattered helmets—Falkirk its broken shields. There were gory lances from Stirling Bridge, and blood-stained swords from Bannockburn—all telling their own tale of rivalry and death. The Earl's heart beat high as he showed his guests the trophies; and as his dark eye rolled from object to object, one would think he felt proud of his descent from the great Dundaff. The ladies played, and the Countess sang, while the chiefs drank their wine; and so the night whiled merrily away. While the nobles laughed and talked, and the rooms rang with the music of the ladies, down in the servants' hall sat a jovial crew. These were the servants of " my lords." Conspicuous in the group was a short and thick well-made form, with long grey hair, dark rolling eye, and countenance brown as the heath on his native moor. That was " Stoat-the-Vrouach," which means, in readable language, · " The Stumpy for the brae," the Earl's archer. Behind him, on the wall, dangled a huge cross-bow and bunch of arrows, with which, in their turn, he had brought down the " enemies of the king " in many a battle-field, the wolf and the stag in the forest, the eagle and ptarmigan on the mountain, and the sea-gull on the lake. In his hand was a long sharp-pointed " sgian-dubh;" the cherished gift of his father, the plaything of his early youth, and the trusty companion of his manhood and riper years. The " Stoat" was a valued servant of the Earl, both on account of his

deeds in the " sgian-dubh" line, and his length of service.
He was long archer to the Earl, and the Earl's son at Dounance. It was at the latter place he performed some of his
most distinguished services, and on one occasion, at least,
saved his master and family from destruction by the M'Pherson. In early times, it is said, one Norman M'Pherson
was laird of Drunkie and Duchray, and was rather a powerful rival to the Menteith family. By-and-by, however,
M'Pherson fell into debt, when he applied to the Earl's son,
at Dounance, to grant him money on his property. Graham
thinking this a good chance of getting M'Pherson into his
grasp, instantly gave him all he asked, under the condition
that, if the money was not paid off by a certain date, the
land should revert to Dounance. M'Pherson failed to fulfil
the conditions, and Graham took hold of Duchray. M'Pherson, driven to despair, retired back on Drunkie, where he
brooded over his revenge, and "nursed his wrath to keep
it warm." After a while, M'Pherson resolved to attack
Dounance, murder the family, and retake Duchray. With
this purpose he left Drunkie with a number of his men,
took Stoat-the-Vrouach prisoner in his own house near
the lake, and ordered the archer to lead the way, at the
same time offering him a large sum to betray Graham into
his hands. The night being dark was well fitted for such
bloody work, and on their arrival all was still within the
castle. " Stand here," muttered the Stoat, " my Lord has
a secret knock which no one knows but myself; I will leave
the door open, and you will rush in at my heels." The
archer stepped forward and gave the secret knock. " What
brings the Stoat here at this time of the night?" asked a

voice from within. "Open: the M'Phersons are at my back; they have come to be revenged for Duchray; make haste, for God's sake! or we are all lost," whispered the archer earnestly. Graham sprung from his couch, the massive door reeled back on its hinges, and another moment saw the Stoat safe within the castle portals. The Grahams were instantly armed, and rushing out upon their foes, made short work of the M'Phersons, who, it is said, were all killed. Norman was pursued by the renowned archer into a cave near to Drunkie House, and there slain, the place being still called "Norman's Wood." The Stoat was delighting his cronies with stories like these, telling them scenes of other days and tales of bygone years; and if the black sgian-dubh he held in his hand could but have whispered, it would have told a tale of its own.

The archer had just finished M'Pherson afresh, when the noise announced the parting of the chiefs, and each valet hastened to the service of his lord; while the Earl's boatmen feathered their oars, ready to row their noble freights over the still waters. There were laughing faces there, and the gentle zephyrs wafted around the fairy island the happy parting, while the echoes whispered back the farewells. The night was calm and clear, as if Nature smiled on the happy gathering. The moon—"pale mistress of the night" —rose as only autumn moons can rise, while the still waters reflected back the glories of a star-pearl'd heaven. The mist crawled along the Braes of Auchyle, and Rednock Hills looked through the grey covering. The lake was quiet as a "mill-pond"—only the zephyrs kissed its waters—no ripple on its bosom save that in the trail of

the scallop; but ever and anon was heard the quack of the
wild drake, startled by the splash of the oar; while far in
the still midnight came the moan of the owl, and

> " The dookers dived beneath the stream,
> And wondered what the thing could mean "

The otter prowled along the shore; the bark of the
fox was heard far off among the dark recesses of Arnmauch; the wild swan spread her wings to catch the floating zephyrs; and the cormorant nestled among the reeds.
When in wine the Earl was fiery and vain—fiery to those
who dared to ruffle his temper, and vain enough to fancy
himself the finest specimen of a man within the Earldom.
As he sat on his couch with the fair young Countess by
his side, chatting over the happy gathering, he suddenly
exclaimed, "Who do you think was the best-looking man
at the ball?" The Countess looked surprised, and smiling,
replied, "What makes the Earl ask such a question?"
"Oh, only for your opinion," replied the Earl dryly.   The
Countess sat closer to the chief, and laying her lily hand
on the shoulder of her haughty lord, whispered into his
ear, "Who but your own kinsman and tenant, Malise
Graham!" and starting from his side, the fair lady glided
away to her bedroom.   For a time the Earl sat in wild
bewilderment, his passion inflamed with wine, and his
brain reeling with the debauch; his brow scowled like the
thunder-cloud, and his eyes stared like fixed stars.   "Malise
Graham," he muttered to himself; and his recollection of
seeing him at several stages of the evening paying close
attention to the Countess, shot through his memory with
meteoric flash.

"Villain!" exclaimed the Earl, "he'll rue those deeds. I'll have his blood before to-morrow's sun rises!" and, clutching his dagger, the jealous lord staggered from his couch breathing curses on his unhappy friend. "Bring me Stoat-the-Vrouach," growled the enraged chief, in tones that rang through every corner of the island; and the only one of the castle who heard not the stern order was the fair Countess, who, close in her bedroom and earnest at her devotions, was all unconscious of the terrible scene about to be enacted, and of which she was the unhappy cause. The faithful archer rushed to the presence of his enraged master. "Go," cried the Earl; "Gloschoil has dared to insult his chief, and this night I have sworn to have his blood; take your men and let him not escape." The old servant looked surprised, and whispered "What means my lord by this? Has the Earl forgotten that his friend is a faithful and true vassal?" "That's for me to judge," cried the Earl fiercely; "do my bidding, and mutter but a rebellious sentence and to-morrow thy carcase shall hang on Miling." With a heavy heart the archer obeyed; and while, with crossbow slung on his shoulder and sword unsheathed, he departed on his mission of death, the half unconscious Earl slunk away to his bedroom. Malise Graham was slowly plodding his homeward path, with neither friend nor guide—he needed none—these hills were the hills of his youth—these his native glens. A thousand times his youthful limbs had trod the breckan brae, when the rocks rang with his boyish voice. Upon yon hill's craggy face he had stalked the red-deer and brought down the eagle; deep in that misty glen he had sought out the wolf, and hunted the wild boar; away.

on the skirts of yonder valley, he had met invading clans, when the clash of shields and the clang of claymores rang wildly around him. Malise's heart was light, he reflected on the happy hours spent with his chief, and the thoughts of his young wife and two prattling boys, that awaited his coming, cheered him on; and as he turned down into his own native strath, there, sure enough, was the light in the window, the traveller's home star. Already he heard the stifled bark of his favourite hound in the kennel at home; that home, alas! he was never to reach. He dreamed not the toils of the assassin, like the serpent's embrace, were drawing closer and closer around him—the Earl's death hounds treading at his heels,—only watching the proper moment for striking the fatal blow. It soon arrived; and as Stoat-the-Vrouach raised aloft his arm, the moon buried her face in a cloud, as if Heaven frowned on the deed; one moment's stillness, and a wild yell burst among the shattered hills and awoke the slumbering echoes of Auchray.*

"What is that, mother?" cried a half-sleeping boy, starting from his pillow, aroused by the dying cry of his father, as it echoed wildly across Loch-Katrine, and rang among the scattered buildings of Gloschoil. "That is father's voice —something has befallen him." "Hush, boy," replied the wakeful mother. "Nothing can befall thy father; the night is clear and the lamp still burns in the window; 'twas the growl of the watch-dog, or the cry of the eagle on the hill. Your father is well acquainted with the track over the hills; the Kittearns know him well; the Macgregors are friendly

---

* A low green mound among the hills, between the Lake of Monteith and Loch Auchray, is still known as "Malise Graham's cairn," marking the spot where he fell.

to the Graham; and the M'Farlanes are thy mother's kinsmen;—there is nothing to fear, and, besides,

> " 'Your father has his favourite sword,
> Made by that man of fame,*
> And woe betide the single arm
> That dares to meet the Graham.' "

And again the boy nestled himself to sleep. 'Twas grey
dawn ere the wife of Malise Graham again looked out of
the window. All was still in the Highland glen; here and
there the curling smoke ascended from the cottars' homes;
the moor-cock was heard on the hill; and the September
hoarfrost lay thick and grey around the shores of Loch-
Katrine, nipping the already fading glories of summer.
The fair lady looked anxious, and whispered to herself,
"My lord is long in coming!"   Then, turning her eyes
towards the "Path of the red post," she saw a number of
men slowly approaching, carrying in their midst an un-
couth looking object. A thrill of fear shot through her
nerves. The anxious wife watched with eager eye, and as
they drew near, she rushed to meet the mournful cavalcade;
and there, sure enough, was Malise Graham, stark and cold,
with the crimson tide oozing from his manly heart. For a
moment the Highland lady surveyed her murdered lord; her
cheek grew pale; her frame shook like a shattered reed; and
with hysteric groan she fell back among her native heather.
And now

> " On Katrine's coast, the widowed dame
> May wash the rocks with tears."

* There is a well-known local tradition that the celebrated sword-maker, Andrew
Ferrara, had an establishment, for the making of swords, at what was once known
as the old Mill of Auchray, long ago a ruin. This may account in some degree for
the number of distinguished swordsmen bred in that district, and we can fancy, in
that dark age, when every glen swarmed with lawless lords, the renowned sword-
maker driving a roaring trade.

On returning to consciousness, the widow's first resolve was revenge; and she determined on rousing her kinsmen, and bringing down on the Earl the vengeance of

"The wild M'Farlane's plaided clan "

But being told of the utter hopelessness of the task, and that there yet remained a cloud of mystery to be cleared away, she abandoned the project.

While this sad scene was being enacted on the heathy shores of Loch-Katrine, another, but of a less terrible description, was going on at the Lake of Monteith. The Earl awoke, as only those who awaken after a debauch can describe. The events of the previous night shot like wild dreams through his brain, and a lingering remembrance of his stern order to the archer floated before his distorted imagination. As he sat looking up to the hill, with the lake calm around him, the door of his room suddenly flew open, and in rushed "The Earl's Niece," the orphaned daughter of the house of Dounance, but not the merry wee thing of former mornings. True, the same blue eyes and rosy cheeks were there, and the flaxen hair hung in its usual silken curls around her neck; but there was a stillness in her eye, and a sadness in her young face, which the Earl could not mistake. The niece was followed by the Countess, also looking sadder than usual. And the Earl, whose mind was haunted by the previous night's events, was trying to banish them as airy phantoms, when he began to see that they were stern realities. In a fit of excitement, he started to his feet, exclaiming, "Is Malise Graham then dead?" "Yes," whispered the Countess; "and the sword of

the archer is gory with his blood." The Earl looked pale;
a scalding tear filled his eye; and he paced the room
impatiently. "What made Stoat-the-Vrouach obey such
foolish orders?" he asked. "The archer remonstrated, and
you threatened to hang him," replied the Countess. "Ay,"
responded the Earl; "pity I did not; but what is done
cannot be undone. I will see to the widow," and he
threw himself back on his couch. The Earl was true to
his promise; he gifted the widow her lifetime of Gloschoil,
and otherwise saw to the well-being of the family, for it is
said he was deeply grieved for the loss of his friend.
Malise Graham had two sons, Malise the elder, and Robert
the younger. Malise was of a mild and gentle nature, and
inherited in a large degree the character of the Grahams.
Robert was a reckless spirit, in fact "a wild M'Farlane,"
and partook deeply of the spirit of the robber clan. All
the wild fancies of youth floated through his brain; the loch,
the glen, and the hill were his favourite delights; and he
loved to rob the eyrie, and possess himself of the young
eagle. He would climb the rocks where no human foot
had ever been but his own, and whose brown surface was
disturbed only by the claws of wild cats, the talons of eagles,
and by a thousand storms. The sea-gull's nests floating on
the bosom of the wide-spreading loch, or hidden among the
reeds of the deep mountain tarn, were alike insecure from
the agile form of Robert Graham. From a mere boy he
bore a mortal hatred towards the Earl; and to be revenged
for his father's death was his only and darling ambition.
During the long wintry nights, when the mother and her
two sons sat by the blazing peat fire in their lone High-

land home, Robert, laying his dark curly head in his
mother's lap, would lisp, " When I grow big I will punish
the Earl for killing my father." . A tear would dim the fond
mother's eye, and she would whisper, " Hush boy, the Earl
is kind; he will one day make you a man."

One day, during midsummer, some years after the death
of Malise Graham, the Earl's niece was sent by the Countess with presents to the widow of Gloschoil. After roaming
for some hours on the banks of Loch-Katrine, Robert was
sent by his mother to see the niece safe over the rugged
" pass of the red post."   Robert felt proud of the honour,
for although he hated the Earl, there was something that
drew him towards the fair young lady he could not describe,
and with light hearts the youthful pair disappeared among
the heather. When Robert and his fair charge left Gloschoil

" Noontide was slumbering on the hill,"

and the lambkins were sporting among the bracken knowes
with hearts as light as their own.   They soon reached
Auchray, when the niece pulled the blue bell, and Robert
gathered the wild clover, to spread on his father's cairn,
while they added a stone each to the heap.   Robert
gazed wistfully at the rude memento of his father's death,
a tear stood in his dark eye, and his heart was full to overflowing; for although Robert was a reckless youth, he had
a large and warm heart, and be he friend or foe, who
trusted in Robert Graham was never disappointed, for his
heart was as good as his nature was rash.   The fair lady
saw the tear that dimmed her young friend's eye, and she
whispered, " 'Twas a sad night that, Robert; but the Earl
repents it deeply." ' Robert was about to break out with

hreats against the Earl; that he would make him rue the
lay he had done the deed;—but the thought of grieving
he niece prevented him, and he concealed the thoughts
n his bosom. Robert saw his fair charge over the hills;
ot parting with her until he put her in sight of her own
airy lake; when bidding her adieu, he turned his steps
omewards to Gloschoil. Years rolled on; Robert grew to
nan's estate, and the hatred towards the Earl grew with
iis years. The canker-worm of revenge gnawed wildly at
iis heart, and, in spite of a mother's warning and brother's
dvice, the youth persisted in cherishing the idea of one
ay revenging his father's blood. In furtherance of his
arling ambition, he enlisted the sympathies of a large
ody of his mother's kinsmen, and other lawless robbers
hat inhabited the wild shores of Loch-Katrine and Loch-
.omond, Robert promising them large rewards. He soon
ound himself at the head of a powerful body of banditti,
ll as eager for the fray as himself, and as earnest to
hare the spoil. The Earl being wealthy, and having a
arge tract of rich country, the hardy half-starved moun-
aineers looked forward to rich rewards. One day, about
wenty years after the death of Malise Graham, the Earl
iad just returned from fishing on the lake, when his eyes
aught the sight of a boat approaching the island from the
iorthern shore. Landing, the messenger handed him a
etter, and then retired as he came. The Earl tore it open.
t was short, but it could not be mistaken; it read thus,—

To the Earl.

"I come to revenge my father's death.

ROBERT GRAHAM."

The old man looked bewildered; and gazed after the messenger, but he had disappeared on the distant shore. The Earl hastened into the hall, not knowing whither he went. For a time he paced the room in a state of wild agitation, as if fully realising the nature of his position; but recollecting himself, he sank calmly back on his seat. At that moment the niece chanced to enter the room, and seeing the sad countenance of her friend and benefactor, she playfully asked its cause. "Ah! and well I might look sad!" replied the Earl. "To-night, I am a dead man; and God knows but you'll be houseless and homeless. Robert Graham of Gloschoil has come to be revenged for his father's death." "That cannot be," exclaimed the maid, and snatching the letter she rushed to the Countess with the fatal epistle. There was no time to lose, the shades of evening were gathering fast around the lake, and already the voice of the foemen came from Crockmelly. The sound of the *slogan* was distinctly heard, and the cry of "Loch Sloy" echoed wildly across Portend. "I'll tell you what to do," whispered the Countess. "Go and meet Robert Graham unarmed; take your niece along with you; offer her to him for wife; and for dowry grant him a portion of land." The Earl, acting on the advice of his wife, met his young and fierce kinsman on the shore of the lake. The old chief first broke silence. "Robert Graham!" he exclaimed, "you have come to be revenged for your father's death?" "Yes," answered Robert. "I hope you will forego your intention," replied the Earl. "Never," growled the youth. "I am getting old now," continued the Earl; "and I know you will not shorten the waning life, nor make my wife a widow." "You made my mother a widow, and me fatherless," cried the passionate boy. "I did," replied the Earl; "and it grieved me to the heart. But I did what in me lay to make amends for it, and I am ready to do more now. Only give up your intention, become peaceful, and I will give you that young lady for your wife, with land for her dowry." "What!" exclaimed Robert, "I become your vassal? No, and I could not protect you now though I were willing,—for

> " Heard'st thou not that loud a-hoy?
> And yonder distant cry ' Loch Sloy'?
> A hundred spearmen, like a tide
> Come rushing down the deep lake side;
> And loudly each for vengeance calls
> To lordly homes and ruined walls."

As the youth finished the last sentence, the niece sprang from the Earl's side, and throwing her arms around the neck of Robert Graham, exclaimed, "Oh, for my sake, Robert, save the Earl!" Her tears bathed his bosom, and her flaxen hair hung in silken tresses on his breast. Robert started, the appeal reached his heart, and the remembrance of the time when she pulled the bluebell, while he gathered the wild clover to spread on his father's cairn, shot with meteoric flash through his memory. The young heroic soul was moved, the naked sword was sheathed, and his men were signalled back from the hill. A short time thereafter Robert Graham became the husband of the Earl's niece, and received as her dowry the lands of Bruchorn in Aberfoyle.

Robert Graham and the Earl's niece lie in the lone island of Inchmahome—the green sod resting lightly on their bosoms, while zephyrs play around their grave; and although the storms of a hundred years have rattled over

E

them, their descendants still live, and many respectable families in Monteith trace with pride their descent from the Earl's niece.

TALLA.

THE island of Talla is the second island in size on the Lake of Monteith. It signifies "A hall," or " Great man's house," but is more commonly known as " the Earl's isle." This island contains the principal stronghold of the Earls of Menteith, now in ruins. Being situated near the middle of the lake, it must in early times have been able to set all attacking forces at defiance. Kilbride Castle, near Dunblane, was, long ago, another of their seats. Robert and Murdo, Dukes of Albany, were also Earls of Menteith, and had Doune, Falkland, and Tantallan Castles. Airth Castle seems also to have belonged to the Menteith family, who were Earls of Menteith and Airth. In Loch-Ard, in Aberfoyle, there are two small islands; on the larger, named "St. Malloch," there were formerly the ruins of a small church or chapel; on the other, which is much smaller, may be seen the remains of a strong building, traditionally assigned to the ambitious-minded Stewart, Duke of Albany. The latter is still known as " the Duke's island," its Gaelic name being " Dundochill." There is a well-known tradition in the district that it was from this island the Duke was taken on the night previous to his execution on the Castle-hill of Stirling; and this tradition is strengthened by the fact that Graham of

Duchray refers to it, in his account of the parish of Aberfoyle, written about 150 years ago, and still preserved in
the Advocates' Library. The castle of Talla, or at least a
considerable part of it, which appears to have been built
with part of the ruins of the church of Inchmahome,
was originally very strong, having covered the small island
on which it is built. The tower and highest portion of
the castle seem to have been chiefly composed of round
stones; and the remains of three storeys are still visible,
hanging their grey and shattered corners over the blue
waters which wash the foundation. The lower portion
was originally divided into three apartments. In the low
storey was "the hall," which measures 16 by 6 paces;
and from an inventory made in the year 1692, and
preserved among the "Menteith Papers" in Gartmore
House, it is said to have been furnished with a "pair of
virginals," as also with "my lord and ladye's portraits, and
hangings before them," and "ane house-knock, with the
caise thereof," &c. The fire-place still remains, and is
perfectly visible. At either end, and in upper storeys,
entered respectively by a door in the gable, and not
encroaching on the ground floor, was a room, each containing a "standing bed and other corresponding furni-
ture." A small tower stands behind the hall, with which
it had a communication, and originally contained three
rooms, each in a storey by itself, the highest having been
reached by a winding stair at the south-west corner.
The middle room, according to the inventory, was "my
lady's chamber." The ground floor is called the "laigh
back room." "The brew-house chamber" was situated on

the east side of the island, and was "hung with green," besides being furnished with two beds, "one of green stuff, with rods and panels to conform; the other of red scarlet cloth." On the west side of the island was the servants' apartments, the kitchen, and oven. Speaking of the oldest portion of the castle, M'Gregor Stirling says:—"Its heraldic devices are partly abstracted, and no account can be given of its foundation, nor indeed of that of any of the more modern structures. From one of these devices, where the crest represents, as is believed, an eagle *caupe*, above a shield, the crest of which is not legible, it would appear the oldest building was erected after the introduction of the first-mentioned emblems into armorial bearings."

A few hundred yards to the west of Talla, lies "the Dog island." This small island is not many yards in circumference, but appears to have been large enough to be used in the Earl's time as a kennel. On the western shore of the lake stood the Earl's stables, long ago razed to the ground: the point of land on which they originally stood is still called "the stable ground." On the northern shore of the lake, and around the beautiful hill of "Coldon" or "Cowden," and on the farm of "Portend," were the pleasure grounds of these noblemen. Here a considerable number of large and beautiful trees still gracefully spread their noble branches over the ancient walks of those feudal lords. Within this pleasure park, and on what is known as "the Friars' meadow," there is still to be seen a considerable mound, said to be consecrated earth brought over from Ireland for holy purposes connected with the church of Inchmahome.

CHAPTER IN THE LIFE OF ROB ROY.

THE morning had dawned on Aberfoyle early in July of the year 1710; and the eastern sun had just burst forth in all the glory of his summer splendour, throwing his golden tints far among the magnificent hills of the country of the Macgregor—when Rob Roy looked out of his cave in the rock-built walls that skirt the western shores of the fairy Loch-Ard. As he gazed over the deep waters of the Highland loch, he laid his rough hand on his red beard and shook the dew from his curly locks; he looked eastward towards the red sun, and westward toward the grey cloud that hung around the top of his native Ben-Lomond. There was no stir in the Pass of Aberfoyle, save among the warbling throng and beasts of prey. On the distant shore trotted reynard; while the otter dashed through the blue waters after its finny prey; behind him prowled the wild-cat deep among its native heather; and above him was heard the cry of the wild eagle as it surveyed the nether air, or floated away to the dizzy cliffs over deep Loch-Chon. There was no sign of life among the honest natives; but as the mist rolled off each rugged glen, the curling smoke might be observed ascending from a dozen smugglers' stills; while on the watch-rock might be seen the rustic form of a

Highlander gazing wistfully down the pass, looking for one whom he hoped not to see, namely, the dreaded "gauger." Macgregor had not looked long on the fairy scene before him till he had matured his plans for the day; and turning back into the cave where his young son lay, with no covering but his Highland kilt, and with the granite rock for his pillow, "Rab!" whispered the Highland chief. Young Rab snored. "Rab!" again muttered the outlaw; but Rab only rubbed his red eyes and turned himself on his hard pillow. "Rab!" again growled the undefeated hero, in a voice of thunder that rang through the dark recesses of the cave, and the echoes from the distant shore whispered it back. The sleeper sprung from his hard bed and clutched his sgian-dubh, but only to confront his angry father. "Get ready," whispered Macgregor. The boy sheathed his dirk, and the rocks rang with the gathering notes of the bugle; when, instantly, a score of hardy natives of the hill and glen sprung from their heathery beds, all eager to do the bidding of their chief. As the sound of the bugle echoed far among the shattered rocks of the Glasshart, the watcher started and gazed wildly down the glen; and here and there might be seen the curly head of a smuggler as he peeped from his still, fancying himself surrounded by a score of rangers. Rob Roy and his party having had a fire kindled on the rock overhanging his cave, were enjoying their morning repast. A good Highland wether, snatched the night before from a flock on the neighbouring hill, had been roasted on the red embers, and the bold but warm-hearted Macgregors might have been seen picking the bones on the heath-clad shores of Loch-Ard.

" I'll pay these refractory lairds a visit to-day!" exclaimed
Rob. "It's not for me to be done this way. I have
not pocketed a penny of black-mail for nearly a twelve-
month; but if I don't teach them a lesson this day, my
hair's not red nor my name Macgregor!" "You mean Auchentroig, I suppose?" asked young Rob. " I do," answered
the chief; "and some of his neighbours also." "Is that
Garden?" asked one of the party. "Yes," replied Rab; "and
I have an old account to settle with the gudeman of Kepdowrie." "What is that?" eagerly inquired the youth.
"Well," continued Macgregor, "a few years ago, when you
were a mere boy, and only able to attend to your father's
flock, or harry the eagle's nest at Inversnaid—at that time I
was engaged in a quarrel I had with the Montrose; and as
I could not be there myself, I sent a score of my best lads
on a lifting excursion to the vale of Strathendrick, and as I
had not been to that country for some time, I expected a
good drove. My men, however," continued Rob, "passed
the gudeman on their way south, who, suspecting their intentions, sent a messenger on horseback to warn his friends
on the Endrick that the Macgregors had passed southwards.
Acting on the hint, the men of the Endrick were hastily
gathered, and led by big Jock Din of Fintry, (curses on
his carcase!) met, outnumbered, and overpowered the
Highlanders, near Balgair. My men fled towards Boquhan
glen, hotly pursued; and big Jock coming up to two of
them, was about to strike one down with his heavy leaden
staff, when my lad instantly wheeled round, and levelled his
piece at his pursuer, but the gun missed fire, when he and
his companion were instantly felled to the earth by the

powerful arm of Din.*   Big Jock then rushed to the
head of the glen, gave one wild cry, that rang among
the rocks like the roar of a lion, and reaching even to
Boquhan, it aroused the Cunninghams, who renewed the
attack, when seven more of my brave lads were slain."
"And so you have good reason to settle accounts, I guess,"
replied several of the gang.   "No doubt," continued
Macgregor; "one member of a rival clan has a good right
to inform his friends of the intended attack of another; but
as I want a year's black-mail, if he is not inclined to cash
up to-day, we shall have the pleasure of his company, and
all that he possesses, to Inversnaid to-night."   "I should
rather think so," chimed in young Rob, as he pitched the
last bone of "the wether" into deep Loch-Ard; and the
gang in general buckled on their swords, wiped the grease
from their grizzly beards, and prepared to "bundle and
go."   "We go straight to Auchentroig," cried Rob, as he
snatched his broadsword—that sword which had taken the
noted freebooter out of a hundred frays, and left him unscathed, while his rivals lay dead around him; "thence towards Garden, pass the night at the Kepp, and, God willing,
return with the spoil to-morrow."   Rob Roy and his hardy
band then started to pay the "refractory" lairds what afterwards turned out not to be a friendly visit, and to claim
that to which, if he had not a right, he by might had a
title.   When Rob Roy left the shores of Loch-Ard on that
somewhat eventful morning, the July sun rose clear and
beautiful, the mist had just left the lesser hills of the Grampians standing clear in bold outlines, and was taking a

* Their two graves are still to be seen.

lingering farewell of the craggy summit of Ben-Lomond. On his right lay classic Duchray, famous in the everlasting pages of history, on whose heather hills the standard of the Graham was unfurled, when the brave vassals gathered around their loyal chief to defend the interests of their injured King. Duchray, with its grey castle and hoary strongholds, its ivy-mantled turrets and dark dungeons, its rocky passes and ferny glens, its deep pools and meandering streams—where the quiet linn contrasts with the roaring waterfall, and the heathery plain with the towering rock, and

> " Here, perched on some o'erhanging rock,
> Far from huntsman's murdering shock—
> On some wild cliff that nears the sky—
> The falcon rears her young on high,
> And feeds with care her tender brood;
> Drops from above the dainty food;
> A moment looks; then, circling round,
> Seeks anew the hunting ground;
> Then, far aloft, with outspread tail,
> She scorns the keeper's leaden hail."

As the Macgregor marched along the heathery banks of the Ard, the loud echoes of the waterfalls were heard deep in the glens, and the dancing spray glittered in the morning sun like a shower of gold.

> " For o'er thy crags, with sullen gush,
> The crystal waters loudly rush;
> And dashing o'er, with deafening shock,
> Plunges on the granite rock.
> Then winding on, both clear and cool—
> Eddying round each silver pool—
> Till with the Duchray rushes forth
> The parents of the infant Forth."

On his left stood the rocky Craigmore, with the wrecks of a thousand storms at its base, and the ravens floating round its summit. The sheep were bleating on the knowes, while the lambs played in the meadows, and the fragrance of the bluebell was wafted far on the wings of the zephyrs. Before him now rolled the dark waters of the Avendhu, with the finny tribe sporting in its deep pools, and the playful fawn on its mossy banks. Rob Roy and his gang strode onwards, chatting over past exploits, and hopefully looking to the future. Approaching Craiguchty, and at a turn of the road, they stumbled on a camp of native gipsies. An old cove, who had grown grey in the service, was striking his tent, and otherwise preparing for the day's campaign. Beside him on the road stood a gipsy girl, covered with what had once been clothes, with brown face and matted hair; on her head the wreck of a cap, an infant on her back, and black pitcher in hand. Perched on a stone sat the female parent stem, with withered hands and wrinkled face, cracking the lice on a young tinker's rags. Defiling through a pass in the hills, Macgregor saw approaching some thirty "flaskers," with cudgels in their hands and unlawful treasure on their backs, marching on towards Glasgow to dispose of the smuggled whisky.

Macgregor and his party concealed themselves behind a knoll, and watched the flaskers approaching. As they drew near, Rob could observe a band of determined looking fellows, powerful and well armed—each having a heavy oaken stick in his hand, and all carrying knives,—just such a lot of men as would face a body of rangers, or a troop of red-coats, regardless of life or limb, provided the darling treasure on their backs was safe; and woe betide the unhappy gauger who should have the misfortune to fall in their way. As the " flaskers" came full round in view of the Macgregor party, Rob gave one wild halloo, that rang among the rocks, sent the sheep bounding up the hill, and brought the whole gang to a stand-still. " In the king's name, surrender!" cried Rob. " Hang me if I will!" roared back the leader of the flaskers; and shouting out, " Gaugers! men!" thirty flasks were rolling on the heath and as many cudgels brandishing in the air, and with earnest hearts prepared to defend, against all comers, the darling "wee drappie." A loud laugh burst·from Rob's men, as they witnessed the confusion into which the smugglers were thrown. " Confound you, Macgregor!" cried one of the flaskers, "we took you for gaugers." " I'll be easier put off than these gentry," replied Rob; " I'll only ask a part of the goods—not all, as gaugers would do." "We are only proud to supply you," responded half-a-dozen voices; and Macgregor and several of his party had their flagons filled; when, bidding each other god-speed,

" They wended each their several way,
In hopes to meet some ither day."

Approaching Auchentroig, the Macgregors were observed by some of·the servants, who immediately informed the Baron of the advance of armed men to the house. Being well aware of their intentions, the Baron proceeded to barricade the doors and windows, to prevent the possibility of their being forced open. The front door was made of red oak, of the most massive description, and filled at regular intervals with strong iron bolts having large round heads, to prevent, if possible, any chance of its being burned. Rob Roy drew up his men in front of the house, and called upon

the inmates to surrender. "Surrender to whom?" cried the
Baron. "To Rob Roy Macgregor!" was the bold reply.
"Never!" quoth the Baron. "Never will the Baron of Auchentroig yield to robber such as thee; and had I had time
to collect my men, one half of your cowardly gang would
never return!" "Force that door!" roared Macgregor; and
instantly a dozen of his men were at it with their brawny
arms, but they might as soon have attempted the mountain
rock. "Fire it, then!" growled the enraged freebooter; and
instantly the torch is applied; but for a time the massive door
defies their efforts. By-and-by, however, the fire catches, and
the bolts fall out one by one, and then there ensues a scene
of exultation and sorrow. Outside ring the jeers and coarse
laughter of the Macgregors; inside is heard the curses of the
Baron, the shrieks of the children, and the stifled sobs of the
ladies. The women, in despair, clamour to let them in. The
Baron rushes forward, seizes the iron-bar, in a moment the
door, black with smoke and red with flame, reels back on
its hinges, and the Baron is a prisoner. The Baron still
refused to settle with Macgregor, and Rob handed him
over to his men to carry him to Aberfoyle; at same time
ordering a party of his men to sweep the estate of the
cattle and sheep—an order which was carried out to the
very letter. An old member of the house of Auchentroig
used to say, "They left not one hoof behind them." The
Baron was kept for some days till Rob's return, when the
ransom was paid, and he returned to his family. The
cattle, however, were never returned, which must have
been a great hardship. An old farmer, who died within the
memory of some parties now living, used to tell, that when

he was a boy herding his father's cattle at Clashmore, near
Gartmore, he saw the Macgregors passing with the Auchentroig cattle, and he used to remark that among the drove
was a fine young grey mare.   He also remarked that the
men were very kind to him—"gave him a lash o' drink,
an' lots o' cake and cheese," a luxury he rarely enjoyed at
home.

After instructing his men regarding the disposal of the
unfortunate Baron and his cattle, Macgregor, with a number of his men, went to settle matters with the guidman of
Kepdowrie, as before arranged.   Here, as well as at Auchentroig, Rob had the misfortune to be seen approaching,
and preparations were made for resistance.   The house at
that time was one of those low one-storeyed buildings, the
outer door opening in two halves inwards.   Built into the
wall was a heavy piece of oak, several inches square, which
drew out behind the door at pleasure, and which made invasion from that quarter impossible.   On the approach of
Rob, the guidman, who was then very old, but still of great
strength, armed himself with what is known in country
districts as "a peat spade," a most unhappy weapon in the
hands of any powerful man, and took up his position behind the door. Presently Macgregor arrived, and demanded
admittance. Getting no answer, he became impatient, and
cried "Who's there?"   "I'm here," coolly whispered the
guidman. "Let me in," cried Rob.   "I will not," was the
reply.   "Come, hand me that siller!" demanded the freebooter. "Not a plack," was the cool response. Rob, getting very angry, dashed at the door, seized the handle,
and made the fabric rattle on its hinges. "Cross but that

threshold," cried the veteran, "and I shall cleave your red head to the shoulders." Macgregor staggered back amazed; and an old rhyme says that

> " Macgregor at the door did stand,
>   And swore like ' Rab the Ranter;'
> The auld man, wi' his spade in hand,
>   Did cheerie up his chanter.
> ' Come in, man, Rab! don't look sae douse,'
>   The auld man he did cry;
> ' There's no ae soul within this house
>   But this peat spade and I.'"

" By the Lord," roared Rob, " and there's one too many !" And, ordering his men off, he left the guidman to his reflections. Rob, not to be done, however, surprised the guidman next day, and carried him and his neighbours of Easter Kepdowrie prisoners to Gartmore, where, promising to cash up for the future, he left them to return home.

After being paid in "peat spade coin" by the guidman, Rob continued his march towards Garden. The then house of Garden stood on a small eminence, a little to the north of where the present mansion now stands, in what was at that time a small lake, but now converted into a beautiful and fertile meadow. The building was of the circular tower kind, the walls being very strong, and, when surrounded on all sides by deep water, must, in early times, have been impregnable. The principal entrance to the tower was by a drawbridge, leading towards the north, and connected with an avenue that is still called "The Causeyhead," a number of the old trees being still growing. On Macgregor's arrival at the castle, he ordered his men to open the drawbridge, to prevent any surprise, while he himself deliberately walked into the hall. "Is the laird at home?" demanded Rob of the servant. "He is not, just now," was the prompt reply. "Do you tell me the truth or a lie?" cried Rob. "I tell thee the truth," retorted the servant sharply. "Well, I shall see," muttered Macgregor; "and if you do not, I shall hing you by the heels from the balcony window." The servant rushed to the door to call assistance to expel the intruder, but was surprised to find the house surrounded by armed men, when he became painfully aware of the character of his visitor. Presently Rob stalked at pleasure through each room in the house, peering into every corner, looking for the absent laird, or anything else worth, should he not find the object of his search. Looking out at one of the windows of the upper storey, he saw the laird and his lady slowly walking down the avenue, and he coolly awaited their approach. "What men are these?" asked the lady of her husband, as they drew near the house, and saw Rob's men marching around it. "Good heavens!" exclaimed the laird, "that's the Macgregors, and there is no other than Rob Roy himself looking out of the window!" As they approached the drawbridge, Macgregor cried, "You have long refused me my reward of protection, Garden, but you must render it now." "I will not," cried the undaunted laird; "I never had protection from you, and you never shall have reward from me." "You shall rue it, then," growled Rob in accents that made the pass ring with their echoes. "I never shall," cried back the laird; "you will not have a penny from me." Macgregor made no reply, but rushing into the nursery, seized a child from the nurse,

and dashing out on the balcony, held, with his long orang-
outang-like arm, the child far in mid air, and swore he
would plunge it in the gulph below, if they would not instantly comply. The laird still refused, well knowing that
Rob would disdain to injure a helpless babe; the lady,
however, as soon as she beheld her infant heir sprawling
between heaven and earth (the cries of the boy and the
curses of Rob Roy mingling in awful contrast, being too
much for any mother to bear), burst out with hysteric yell,
"Garden is at your will; only save my son!" Macgregor
being made sure of his protection money, ordered the drawbridge to be lowered, and the laird and his lady admitted
to the house. After being paid the full amount claimed
by him, Rob handed his tender charge over to his affrighted
mother, bestowing a Highland benediction on the laird, and
advising him to be more attentive to his just debts for the
future, lifted the drawbridge to prevent pursuit, and set
off for Amprior, where he intended to pass the night.
Rob Roy and his men took up their quarters in the only
public-house in the village, and prepared to make themselves comfortable after the day's fatigues, by indulging in
a little of the mountain dew. Captain Cunningham, of
Boquhan, chanced to be in Amprior on the same evening,
accompanied only by a friend and his servant, and, un-
aware of the presence of the Macgregors, stepped into the
house. A short time previous to this there existed a deadly
feud between Rob and Cunningham, on account of a severe
chastisement a party of Rob's men received at the hands
of Cunningham. They had met, however, on one occasion
before this, and although by no means friendly, they were

F

certainly on better terms. Cunningham, who was a retired officer, was a tall and handsome man, rather more sinewy than powerful-looking, and acknowledged to be the best swordsman in the King's service, he having put to flight an Italian who challenged the English army. Besides being a skilful swordsman, he was gifted with great stretch of arm, and had a peculiar squint, which, while it rather dumfoundered his antagonists, often proved of great service to him. On Cunningham entering the room, Macgregor exclaimed, "Glad to see you, Cunningham." "Halloo, Rob Roy!" was the reply. "What's up to-day?" "Not much," answered Rob. "I have just been calling on your neighbour laird, and I guess his lady will not ask to see my red face this twelve-month." "Rob Roy Macgregor does not mean he has done anything serious to the lady?" replied Cunningham. "Not at all," quoth Rob; "I only frightened her a little." "Take the other side of that table," cried Macgregor; "it's a while since you and I met in such friendly quarters." "Proud to do so, and ready to face you at all times," cried the free and warm-hearted Cunningham; at the same time shaking Rob warmly by the hand. Rob shrugged his shoulders as if he did not altogether relish the word "ready," but made no reply. There sat the two proud and warm-hearted chieftains in the little front room of the "corner house" at Arnprior, quaffing their reeking punch, and "fighting their battles o'er again." At each side of the table sat the outward friends, but inward rival chiefs; while round the room sat the rustic Highland corps.

> " There each the social cup did quaff,
>   Each mingled in the merry laugh.

> There sat the lawless, dauntless corps,
> Their former battles fought once more
> On went the fun, as each declared
> How many fights and spoils he shared—
> How many foes he'd put to flight—
> When standing up in single fight—
> How each came out free skaith from harm,
> By dint of skill and strength of arm.
> Macgregor told, in long detail,
> His grand exploits when levying mail:—
> He'd viewed the prey with eagle eyes,
> Had caught his victims by surprise;
> He'd rushed, like wolf from out his den,
> And seized upon thy heir, Garden;
> He'd, like a deluge, with his staff
> Swept the hill country round Dundaff.
> He'd oft been proud to check the pride
> Of haughty chiefs on Lomondside;
> He'd met Argyle and faced Colquhoun,
> And waged war with clansmen round.
> Oft had he, to speed his fame,
> Measured lances with the Græme."

"I understand," cried Macgregor, addressing Cunningham, "you had a set-to with an Italian?" "I had a slight brush," replied Cunningham. "Tell us it," cried half-a-dozen voices at once. "Well," continued the Captain, "immediately before I left the King's service, an Italian landed in England, who had been creating a great sensation on the Continent by his extraordinary feats of the sword. He had never been defeated, and, in fact, had either killed or maimed all who opposed him. Landing at London from France, where he had defeated some of the most expert swordsmen of that country, the fellow had the audacity to challenge the British army! For a time there was no response; as no one seemed to have the courage to face the undefeated foreigner. Seeing the dishonour that would accrue from the non-acceptance of such a challenge, I resolved to meet him myself and abide the issue. We did meet, and he seemed a terrible foe— tall and strong, and carrying the most awful-looking sword you ever beheld. As soon as I saw him prepared, I suddenly sprung upon the stage, swung my sword out at full length, and stared him wildly in the face, calling him to come forward. He advanced one or two steps with a bold and careless air, when he suddenly stopped, and surveying me from head to foot, stood for a moment as if paralysed; then, sheathing his sword, he uttered a most hideous yell, and fled from the stage;—thus ended my meeting with the Italian." "Hurrah for the Sassenach!" burst from a dozen Highland throats, as Cunningham finished his story, while his health was pledged in as many drained tumblers. "Then, Captain," cried Macgregor, "it was that squint of yours, and not your sword, that frightened the poor Italian." "Then, Rob Roy, was it that squint that makes the bones of seven of your men lie bleaching on the banks of Boquhan Glen?" "What! do you know whom you insult?" roared Macgregor, as he started to his feet and clutched his dagger. "I do," replied Cunningham, starting from his chair and confronting the outlawed chief. "Where is your sword, and I will teach you a lesson?" growled Macgregor. "That's what no Macgregor ever could do," returned Cunningham. Cunningham, having come unarmed, had sent his servant home for his sword; his family, however, suspecting some foolish broil, refused to give it, and he returned without it. Observing an old sword in a corner of the room, the Captain instantly dashed at it, and insisted on fighting. Macgregor put his back to the wall, and swept his sword around him. Cunningham ordered him to the field in front of the house; an order which he reluctantly obeyed. It was early morning when these two rival chiefs rushed to the glen-side of Arnprior, to seek each other's blood. The eastern sun had just burst forth in more than summer brightness, was casting golden tints along the braes of the Kepp, and revealing the hidden beauties of the lowland glen. No stir, save the murmur of the stream, as it played among the ferny rocks, till the clash of swords— as those two warriors, mad with jealousy and their eyes red with wine, rushed at each other with wild-cat fury—awoke its slumbering echoes. But the ever sagacious Rob Roy found, at the very first onset, that he was no match for him who had been

"Trained abroad his sword to wield,"

and instantly dropping his blade, held out his hand to Cunningham, who grasped it warmly. The two again returned to "the Corner," where they drank till far on in the afternoon—a practice prevalent in Arnprior till the present day.

In the month of August of the year 1691, Rob Roy, then in the pride of his youth and zenith of his fame, encouraged by a desire for plunder, emboldened by successes, and undeterred by a feeble government, headed what is called in local history "The herriship of Kippen." The daring Macgregor on this occasion is said to have been followed by a band of marauders five hundred strong. It does not appear that this was a raid on Macgregor's own account; and Mr. Macgregor Stirling, in his notes to the "History of Stirlingshire," says,—" This was nothing more than a military diversion in favour of his legitimate Sovereign;"—a sentence, it must be confessed, I cannot fully comprehend. At the head of this large and daring band, Rob swept the country around Balfron, the valley of the Endrick, and the whole western half of the parish of Kippen, at his will; lifting horses, cattle, and sheep, and anything else of value he could lay his hands upon. Resistance was impossible. To attack him was madness. The only way of reaching his Highland heart, was to plead poverty. One poor man who had followed him from beyond Balfron to near Gartmore, and there told him a "tale of woe," had his two cattle returned to him. When leaving the village of Fintry, Macgregor saw a man coming along the road with a burden on his back, who afterwards turned out to be a weaver, on the road home with a web of cloth to some of his customers. Riding up to the traveller, Rob asked what he carried. "What's that to you?" replied the fellow. "I'll let you know what's that to me," cried Macgregor; and, springing from his horse, took the traveller by the neck, and gave him such a shake that made his nerves rattle to his very heels. "It's a bit wab," gasped the terrified weaver. "Let's see it," cried Rob. Rob being pleased with the pattern, helped himself to as much as would make a kilt, after which he allowed the weaver to go. Getting the web on his back, he had only proceeded a few yards, when, looking over his shoulder, he exclaimed, "Ye'll answer for that yet, Rab." "Ay, my man, when will that be?" asked Rob. "At the last day," cried the weaver exultingly. "Ye gi'e lang credit, man; I'll just take a pair o' hose," roared Rob; and the unhappy weaver had to submit to a further demolition of the web.

Returning through the western portion of the vale of Monteith, Macgregor and his men halted for the night on the farm of Kinachlachan, about two miles west of the village of Gartmore. Hearing of this incursion, a party of military, or Western Militia, as they were called, then stationed at Cardross House, were ordered out to follow the marauders. There had been some festivities going on at Cardross, and when the soldiers were ordered out they were in no fit condition for the task, the tradition being that they were all more or less intoxicated. As a striking proof of this it is said the officer in command left his quarters with only one round of ammunition per man. Getting notice in the evening that the Macgregors were likely to pass the night to the west of Gartmore village, the commander of the military led his men up the valley of the river Forth, to a point where it is joined by the water of Kelty; then passing up the strath of the latter, he reached the western portion of the Dram of Drumit at early dawn. Under the cover of this ridge he could now see the northern marauders at a distance, making rapid preparations for starting—the rising sun shining brightly on the motley camp. The plundered sheep lay bleating among the heather, the stolen cattle were grazing on the plain; and here and there could be seen a kilted Highlander driving back the wandering steeds. The sound of the bugle had just ran along the Dram, calling the slumbering clansmen to march, when, like startled hares, five hundred kilted warriors sprang from their heathy beds; while, mounted on a hardy steed, and sword in hand, could be seen the giant form of the great freebooter himself. Unperceived, the soldiers crept very near the Macgregors. Rob's own servant, Allister Roy Macgregor, was the first to observe them, and creeping back behind a dyke, shot an advancing soldier dead. This bold stroke on the part of Allister had two very different effects; it woke the Macgregors to a sense of their danger, while it sent a thrill of terror to the hearts of their pursuers. Rob, seeing the military, instantly galloped back to his men, and ordered them to draw their swords. The commander of the soldiers, although seeing the bold attitude of Roy's men, fancied they would flee at the first volley, and ordered his men to discharge their muskets; but instead of daunting the Highlanders they became the more infuriated, and dashing at the soldiers who were now entirely out of ammunition, caused them to flee in the wildest confusion. One of the soldiers engaged Rob single-handed, but finding he was no match for the giant Highlander, he instantly turned and fled. Macgregor galloped after him with the intention of cutting him down, when the soldier suddenly stooped, tore a heavy shoe from his foot and hurled it with great violence at his pursuer, which striking Rob upon the breast, nearly threw him from the saddle. Seeing a man mowing grass in a field close by, the soldier rushed behind him and craved protection. Rob came up and demanded his surrender. "Never," cried the man of the scythe. "Do you know," roared Rob, "that I am Rob Roy Macgregor? And I have sworn an oath that no red coat shall stand this day." "I care not for your oath," returned the noble-hearted peasant; "but," continued he, and turning to the soldier, "I'll relieve him of his oath. Put off your coat, and put on that of mine."

Then raising his scythe with his brawny arm, he held it far in mid-air, and cried, " Be you Rob Roy, or demon, come but one step further and I shall make your red head dance on the bog!"* Rob gazed for one moment at the awful weapon as it flashed in the morning sun, and reining up his horse, turned back towards the battle-field. A wounded soldier took refuge in ·the-farm-house of Gart-nahodick. The goodwife of the house ran and stood in the door, with her hands resting on either side, when ·a Macgregor came up and demanded admittance. "You may get in," replied the woman, " but it will be through me."† The man did not insist, and thus the soldier escaped. A young boy, the son of an officer, being pursued by one of Rob's men, ran behind some bystanders, and cried wildly to be saved; but the ruthless Highlander dashed at him and shed his young blood on the dark moor of Kinachlachan. Till within a few years the graves of those slain were marked by green spots among the long heath, but with some recent improvements they are now not so easily seen.

This was the most serious misdemeanour Rob Roy was ever accused of. It seriously attracted the notice of Government, and a reward of one thousand pounds was offered for his head. At the same time, large bodies of cavalry were marched into Monteith, Aberfoyle, and other parts of the Western Highlands, to check the lawless chief. Macgregor, however, valued his head far more than the

* This spot is still called " The Soldier's Mollan"—*i e.* meadow.

† Information from Mr. James M'Donald, Gartfarran, whose grandmother was present at the time.

Government could afford to offer for its capture, and after being made aware of the proclamation, he for a time dispersed his band, and, along with a few chosen ones, sought the sweets of retirement among the wild rocks and woods on the shores of his native Loch-Lomond. After a time, and at the intercession of some of Rob's friends, the proclamation was revoked, and Rob was once more a free man.

In consequence of the harsh and cruel treatment Rob received at the hands of Montrose and his factor, he considered it his duty, both to himself and family, to take ample revenge on the authors of his misfortunes; and with this end in view, he was neither slow nor slack when occasion suited. He would, with his "lads," as he was wont to call them, emerge from his rocky fastnesses, like the wild eagle from her eyrie, on his doomed prey, lifting the cattle of his enemy, and sweeping his estates of everything of value for his lawless life. For many years he kept up a regular system of annoyance, and which must have told heavily on the resources of Montrose. Year after year, he called on the tenantry farming the northern portions of the Duke's estate, and compelled them to deliver up the rents then due to his Grace, at the same time taking good care to grant receipts for what he had lifted on the part of the Duke; thus keeping the tenants all right with the factor, and freeing from all responsibility those helpless individuals. Although Macgregor delighted to plunder and annoy Montrose, and the other neighbouring proprietors who refused to pay him the stipulated "black mail," he was the friend of the oppressed, and the ready benefactor of the poor and needy; and many a hard-up tenant did he relieve in the dark hour of adversity, when there was no helping hand but his own. Coming down through Aberfoyle from Inversnaid one day, about the year 1716, and approaching a small farm which was at that time tenanted by a widow of the name of Macgregor, he was rather surprised to see a number of men near the cottage. Being anxious to know what was likely to take place, he and his chosen ones drew their swords and stepped boldly into the house. "What's up with you the day, Mrs. Macgregor?" exclaimed Rob, as he entered. "Oh, Mr. Macgregor," cried the sobbing dame, "I ha'e faun ahin' wi' my bit rent, and the factor's comin' the day tae sell my things, and there the folk gatherin' tae the roup." Rob Roy Macgregor had a heart that could feel for every pang of human distress, and a tear stood in his noble eye as he heard the mournful tale, thought of the horrid oppression, and gazed on the three helpless children, as they clung to their lone mother's knee and cried for bread. "How much are you behind, Mrs. Macgregor?" asked Rob. "I am just twenty pounds," replied the widow. "Oh, is that all?" replied Macgregor cheerily; "I'll soon make you all right—I always carry something in a hugger for folk of your sort;" and, plunging his hand into his long waller purse, he handed the widow the required sum. "And now," said Rob, "you will get a receipt, and leave me to settle with Mr. Graham;" and Rob took his leave, while a thousand benedictions were being showered on his head. Rob Roy and his men concealed themselves in a small public-house that then stood on the roadside near the Gleshard, on the classic shores of Loch-Ard. Presently Graham arrived, and was rather surprised to find the widow prepared to settle his claim. On asking who had been kind enough to help her with the money, the widow replied, "I hope the siller will do you as meikle guid as it's done me, factor." Graham, feeling he was rather cut short, granted the receipt, and, along with his clerk and servant, took his way home. Macgregor, who had all the while been watching the factor's movements, cautiously awaited his opportunity, and, as he drew near, stepped out on the road to meet him. "Well, Graham, how did the sale go on?" cried the sarcastic freebooter. Graham looked daggers, gazing as if he had beheld an apparition; and, seeming fully to realise his position, muttered out, "We had no sale." "Oh, she would settle up, I suppose, then?" returned Rob. "No, she did not," replied Graham, getting afraid of his cash. "Come, come, factor, no more of your lies; I know she did, and hand me my money at once," cried Macgregor, getting somewhat impatient. "I got no money; and, you ruffian, you shall pay for this interference," retorted Graham. "Tell your lies to your master, but not to me," roared Rob Roy; and, dashing at the bewildered factor, clutched him by the ears and shook him like a withered reed, till his screams rang through every glen, and the rocks threw back the echoes. Seeing there was no escape, Graham handed Rob "the widow's mite," being in perfect terror of his life. "Now," said Macgregor, as he pocketed the money, "see you do the like of this no more, for as long as there is life in this heart, nerve in this arm, and steel in this sword, no Sassenach shall dare insult the poor in the country of Rob

Roy. You may trample out the lives of your serfs at Killearn, but not on the soil of the Macgregor."* After this
very sensible advice on the part of Rob, he allowed the
factor to proceed on his way; and, I presume, he would
plod his path to Killearn rather crestfallen.

About this time Montrose had a meal-store at Miling,
a farm on the western shores of the Lake of Monteith; and
when Macgregor was in any strait, this store was of considerable value to him, as it often supplied himself and
his men with a very necessary article. It having come to
the knowledge of Rob Roy on one occasion that a number
of the cottars on the Duke's estate in Monteith were in
rather poor circumstances, he instantly issued orders to a
number of the Duke's tenants to meet him at Miling, on a
certain day, and on horseback. The tenantry, although
rather surprised at this demand, had more sense than
disobey it, and they all met him at the appointed time.
After meeting, Rob asked the names of all the most deserv-
ing poor in the neighbourhood of each of the tenants present, and after being informed on the point, he ordered
the storekeeper to hand over to the men a stated quantity
of meal for each poor family, and desired the tenants to
convey it on the horses' backs to the individuals. At the
same time Rob gave the storekeeper a regular receipt that
the distribution was by order of his Grace, thus keeping
the storekeeper all right as to his accounting for the meal.
The storehouse is still standing, and is carefully preserved
by the noble proprietor.

* Information from Mr. Alexander Miller, Aberfoyle, who had it from an old
man who died about 70 years ago, at a very advanced age, and who knew Rob
Roy in early youth.

.· Whether this "generous" action on the part of Macgregor was solely for the interests of the poor cottars of Montrose, or with a desire to annoy his enemy for the cruel persecution he and his family had received at the hands of his Grace's factor, is not known. One thing, however, is certain, that his great sagacity contrived to make all his transactions clink together for his own interest; and although he was in reality the poor man's friend, yet in most cases he took good care to be no loser by the transaction; and it is said he turned this "raid" into good account, although at the end it very nearly cost him his life. Macgregor, thinking that a little in the cattle-lifting line would be a good finish to the meal transaction, and as it might save him a trip some other time,—made a dash at the village of Gartmore, and succeeded in lifting a number of cattle belonging to the villagers. Among the spulzie were some animals belonging to one Miller, a resident of the village. Miller being himself a bold and daring man, resolved to pursue Rob Roy, and retake his cattle, or perish in the attempt. Accordingly, he armed himself with his dagger and pistol, and, accompanied by a single servant, set out on the hazardous enterprise. Miller tracked Macgregor as far as Glendhu; but there, having lost track owing to the darkness of the night, and being considerably tired by the journey, he resolved to pass the night. Entering the inn (?), Miller and his servant partook of some refreshment, after which they retired to bed, having heard nothing of Rob or the lost cattle—the servant sleeping in front of the bed, and Miller at the back. The travellers had been but a short time in bed, when the trampling of feet, the noise of several voices, and the lowing of cattle were heard around the house. "Do ye hear that, maister?" muttered the servant, at the same time giving his half-sleeping master a punch with his elbow. "What is it?" whispered Miller. "It's the rout o' yer ain stirks," replied the watchful servant. "Keep quiet till we see what will turn up," whispered Miller. In a short time Rob and his men entered the house, having secured the cattle for the night. After some conversation with the landlord, and being regaled with a horn or two of the mountain-dew, Rob asked for his favourite bedroom. In passing to the room allotted to him, Rob had to pass through the one in which Miller and his man lay, and seeing a fire in the grate he stepped forward to light his candle. Hearing some one in the room, Miller raised his head and there beheld the thief of his cattle stooping at the grate. Thinking this was now his opportunity, Miller raised himself gently up, and with nervous arm took aim at the noted freebooter. He drew the trigger, and clack went the hammer; but, alas for the Gartmore hero! the powder only flashed in the pan, and left him helpless. Rob, who was perfectly unconscious of any one being in the room, instantly "smelled powder," and, clutching his pistol, fired, when a yell burst from the dark bed, and Miller fell dead on the pillow.*

Early one May morning in the year 1716, Rob Roy Macgregor, then residing at Glengyle, near the head of Loch-Katrine, ordered into his presence his faithful and trusty servant, Allister Roy Macgregor. Allister was instantly in the presence of his chief, and was at all times

---

* Information from Mr. James M'Donald, Gartfarran.

only too glad to be of service to him. This individual is said to have possessed almost the great sagacity of Rob himself, and being of the true Macgregor stamp, was intrusted by him on many an important mission, and was held in great esteem by his master, as on many occasions his services were of very considerable value. "Allister," said Rob, as the servant drew near, "I am a little hard up, and it is now about the time Montrose's rents are due; and as he has taken the precaution of lifting them privately this last time or two, and that too before they fell due, you will go down to Drymen, and cause to be proclaimed at the church door, on Sunday first, that I have gone to Ireland, and will not be home for some weeks; and this will no doubt induce Graham to collect the rents at once. Before you return, you will, if possible, get word when and where the factor is likely to collect. And now, Allister, be to me as you have been before." "Just leave that to me, chief," replied Allister, proud to be sent on such a mission; and a few minutes after the faithful servant was hurrying down the rugged side of Loch-Katrine on his way to Drymen. Allister reached the village of Drymen late on Saturday evening, and as the people were assembling to the church on the following day, he caused the officer to proclaim at the church door that Rob Roy had gone to Ireland a few days before, on business of great importance, and could not be back before some weeks; and that said proclamation was to inform his friends in that quarter the cause of his absence. Having got this part of the mission completed, Allister stayed that night and the following day and night in the village, but without getting any information regarding

the rent collection. Leaving somewhat early on the following morning, and coming across what is known as the Moor
of Drymen road, leading towards the village of .Gartmore,
and as he turned down the hill, commanding à beautiful
and extensive view of the surrounding country, Allister
stretched himself on the green grass to enjoy the scene.
Before him, in all its varied enchantments, lay the lovely
vale of Monteith—the lake, like a fairy thing, slumbering on
its bosom—and rivers watering its plain,—with the Castle
rock of Stirling and the Abbey Craig looming through the
morning mist, and the Ochil hills filling in the background.
Allister, too, could see the battle-ground of Sheriffmuir, on
whose bloody field he took part only the year before. On
his left, rolled the infant Kelty deep o'er its rocky bed, with
the finny tribe sporting in its dark pools. There, too, lay
the battle-field of Kinachlachan, where, by his own dexterity
and watchfulness, Allister had, when in the full bloom of
his youth, slain an advancing enemy, and saved his master
and spoil from capture. The village of Gartmore lay bask-
ing in the morning sunshine, with its curling smoke rising
far in mid air, while the bald head of the Grampians towered
beyond. On his right was heard the cry of the moor-cock
and the song of the shepherd, mingled with the bleating
of the lambs as they sported among the long heather, or
the bark of the shepherd's dog, as it drove back some wanderer from the flock. Above him was heard the carol of
the lark, as it soared upwards towards the blue vaulted
heaven, and the falcon, with outspread wing, floated over
her eyrie on the Gowlan rock; while the peeweep and the
plover filled the air with their doleful cries.

G

Allister was thus enjoying the sylvan scene, when his attention was attracted to a youth as he came tripping over the heath. The Highlander lay watching his approach, when suddenly, and as if by magic, the youth disappeared among the long heather. Allister started to his feet and gazed in the direction where he was last seen, and presently beheld him floundering up through the heath; and shaking the fog and moss from his shoulders. With the agility of the mountain cat the stripling sprung on to the road, and instantly recognising Allister as the man he had seen at the church-gate on Sabbath, he exclaimed, " Man! I wish Rob Roy, instead of going to Ireland, had come and lifted the Duke's rents, as he's done mony a time before, an' no haen me lost among thae mortal peat holes." Allister instantly picked up the idea, and the thought that he had now fallen on the right scent shot through his brain with meteoric flash, and he eagerly replied, " Did ye say ye was warnin' to the rents?" "Atweel am I; an' I ha'e been knockin' amang cottars an' peat holes the hale mornin'," replied the careless boy. Allister was now fully satisfied that the whole matter could be got by a little extra pumping, and, as they strode on towards the village, he took every precaution to drag from the unsuspecting boy when and where the rents were likely to be collected. " When did ye say the rents are to be gathered? I'm a wee Hielan'; I didna understand you very weel," said Allister. " There's some o' *your* sort no sae very Hielan' after a'; our herd callan's Hielan', and when ye tell him to mind his wark, he looks as if he was as Hielan's the very deevil; but when ye say, ' Its dinner-time, Donald,' he understands ye fine."

Allister laughed deep in his own sleeve, and the boy continued, "The factor's to lift the rents on Friday." "It'll
be at Drymen?" chimed in the cautious Highlander. "No,
it's no; it's to be down there at the Chapelarroch," replied
the youth. "Is there an inn there?" asked Allister. "Yes,"
continued the boy; "an' there's a letter tae the man in the
inn to have the factor's dinner ready for him." "Ay, an'
I'se warrant he'll tak his dinner hearty," replied the Highlander. Approaching the chapel, Allister was anxiously
taking stock of the country, and planning to himself the most
convenient way of surprising the house without being observed; and seeing a considerable quantity of broom growing on the Dram of Drummit, he whispered to his companion,
"There's a good deal of broom on that brae." "Man, an'
it's richt deep," was the quick response. "Will it tak ye ower
the head?" asked Allister. "Ower the head!" muttered the
boy. "If ye were in the middle o't ye wid neither see sun
nor win'." Allister having thus fully satisfied himself on
all the more important points connected with the rent collection, took leave of his young companion, and hastened
on to Glengyle, to inform his chief of his success. The
faithful servant reached home in due time, and recounted
to Rob his adventure with the boy, and the information he
succeeded in drawing from him; when Macgregor at once
determined on seizing the money, and securing the person
of Graham himself. Accordingly, he mustered a strong
band of choice "lads," and marched down through Aberfoyle the night previous to the rent collection; and, to
prevent being observed, he took the moor by Clashmore to
the west of the village of Gartmore. Arriving at a place

called "Balloch Roy," or the "Red Pass," the hardy band
sat down in the early dawn to sharpen their swords. Macgregor and his party next reached the Dram of Drummit
unobserved, and took up their position among the long
broom, where they lay concealed till well on in the afternoon. In this hiding-place Rob had a full view of
the house, and saw all the transactions going on. He
watched with more than eagle's eye the tenantry as they
went to and from the inn. As the day wore on, and the
last tenant had apparently left, Rob thought the convenient time had now come for him to be up and doing, and,
as he always liked to do things in a becoming manner,
he ordered his piper to play before him to the house. On
hearing the sound of music, Graham, who was seated at
dinner, surrounded by a number of the tenantry, started
up to learn the cause, and was thunderstruck to see his
old enemy, instead of being off to Ireland, in the very
act of entering the house. "Good heavens!" exclaimed
Graham, as he beheld Rob, "here's Rob Roy! all's up!"
The roast beef fell from his teeth. "What shall I do
with my money?" cried the factor in despair, and turning as
pale as death. "Throw it into that loft," whispered one
of the tenantry; and instantly the bags containing the collected rents were rattling on the sooty rafters. Macgregor
entered with a bold but careless air, naked sword in hand.
"Come awa, Mr. Macgregor," cried one of the company.
"I'm just coming; I'm one of those folks that require little
treating," replied Rob. "Will you have some dinner?"
asked Graham, anxious, if possible, to get the fair side of
Rob. "I will—I have had a long day o't," was the quick

response; and Rob sat down at the table, thrusting his sword
far ben among the plates. Macgregor and the factor, with
those at the table, made a most agreeable dinner, chatting
over the events of the period, which were then very
stirring, and never once alluding to the rents. Dinner being
finished, Macgregor thought it was about time to begin
business, as the afternoon was wearing on. "Have you
any objections to a tune, factor?" asked Rob. "Not in the
least; would only be delighted with a tune," replied Graham.
Rob instantly ordered his piper to play up a certain tune;
and which he did with stirring effect. This was the precon-
certed signal for his men to surround the house, and six instantly entered the room with drawn swords. The tenants
looked at the factor and the factor at the tenants; and it then
began to dawn on his hardened heart that all was not over.
Starting to his feet, and clutching his sword as if in the act
of leaving, Rob turned to the factor and exclaimed, "By-
the-by, Mr. Graham, how did you get on with the rents?"
"Oh, I have got nothing; I have not yet begun to collect,"
replied Graham. "No, no, chamberlain; your lies will not
do for me. Rob Roy always counts by the book; out with
it," rejoined the hero. The book was accordingly produced;
and it having been seen that the money was collected, it
was instantly ordered up. Graham, shaking like a shattered reed, produced the bags, which were immediately pocketed by Rob, in presence of the dumfoundered chamberlain. "And now, Mr. Graham," continued Macgregor, "it's
a long time since I saw you at Loch-Katrine; ye'll come
along and see how I am getting on there?" "No, no; I
beg pardon; I pray to be excused," muttered the trembling

chamberlain. "You pray to be excused; what effect had the prayers of my Helen on your hardened heart, when you insulted her, drove my children from their home, at Craigroystan, and wrongously seized upon my estate—long the land of the Macgregor? And it shall yet be theirs. There was no pardon for my boys, when you drove them out, helpless, amid the storm, when their father was far away in England, when there was no helping hand for the Macgregor, and no mercy with the Graham. Now there shall be no mercy with the Macgregor. Allister, seize him! I will settle with the rogue when I get him to the shores of Loch-Katrine."

These last words of Rob Roy were delivered with a sternness of character that told he meant what he really spoke. Graham understood them well; and he looked anxiously around him, but there was no helping hand there. He well knew that to attempt resistance was to annihilate the only hope of saving his life, and he resolved at once (though he deserved none) to throw himself on the mercy of his captors; and, quivering like an aspen leaf, the bewildered chamberlain crawled from the dinner-table at Chapelarroch more dead than alive. "Play up a tune," cried Macgregor to his piper. "He'll be the first Graham ever was played up the Boreland brae." The order was instantly obeyed, and the Macgregors pushed on their way to Loch-Katrine, with the crestfallen factor in their front, cheered only with the stirring strains of the bagpipe. As he passed the village of Gartmore, and entered the dark defiles of the Highland mountains, Graham's heart almost sank within him. On either side were frowning hills and

yawning glens; above him towered the rocks, as, like
naked skeletons, they hung in shattered masses over his
unhappy head; beneath him roared the waterfall, as it
foamed over its rocky bed; behind him the sun was fast
sinking below the western horizon; before him he saw the
shades of evening gathering around the hill-tops of the
Trossachs, and on either side the mist began to wade
among the stinted hazel, and to linger on the bosom of
Loch-Auchray; while here and there a twinkling star could
be seen high up in the heavens, telling plainly that night
had already began "to tread the heels o' day." Alone,
in a wild and lawless country, with foes on every side,
Graham now began to reflect on his sad position. He
had shown but little mercy himself; and now he could
look for none. In front strode Rob Roy, the sworn
enemy of his master; on either side were his trusty retainers, with drawn dirks; while at his back was Allister, with
a naked sword. Graham felt that his life hung by a single
thread. One word of Rob could set him at liberty—another
send his carcase to feed the eagles; and the bewildered
chamberlain knew not but the first rock might be his block,
or the first tree his gibbet. Rob Roy strode onwards
before his captive in sullen silence; and, reaching Loch-
Katrine, Macgregor, in a voice that echoed far across the
loch, sending the wild drakes quacking from the reedy
inlet, ordered Graham into a boat, and his men to pull
him to the island. The men pulled away through the deep
waters of Loch-Katrine, Graham knew not whither.
Around him in the boat were his sullen captors. Silent
also sat the captive, as he gazed out on the ruffled waters,

and looked around him on the wild Highland scene.
Above him in solemn grandeur towered the shaggy form of
Ben-Venue, its bald head hidden by a cloud, and its black
shadow lying far across the loch. Among the rugged hills
was seen the blaze of the heather, as, like some mighty serpent, it hissed and darted its fiery tongue among the long
heath, and spread its red wing on the breeze, sending its
fiery glare high into the clouds. The shallop, steered by
brawny arms, sped on through the still waters; and as they
neared the island, the darkness was deepened more by the
shades of the thick copsewood. Bounding away among
the dark recesses, was heard the light foot of some startled
deer, while from the forest came the wail of the tawny
owl, as it floated after its evening prey; and as the piercing
cry rang in his ears, Graham fancied it the last howl of
some dying captive less fortunate than himself. Before he
had time to reflect, the boat struck on the rocky island, and
a gruff voice ordered him on shore. Crawling out among
the rocks, the half-dead factor found himself on a lonely
island on the "Loch of the Robber." "Follow me," cried
Macgregor sternly, as he led the way to Graham's future
prison-house. The captive moved on in Rob's track, and
rising above the thick underwood he saw looming before
him a gloomy ruin, dismal and dark as the forebodings of
his own soul. "Put him in the old room, Allister," cried
Rob Roy, "and set two of the lads to keep watch and
ward over him till I settle matters with him in the morning." The faithful servant bowed to his chief, and led his
charge up a short flight of steps, and along a dark and
narrow passage—the only light being that of the moon, as

it glimmered through the broken roof. A few more steps, and Graham found himself within a dreary-looking abode. A cold shiver shot through his whole frame as he sank down exhausted on a broken stool, while Allister turned the key in the rusty lock, and retraced his steps down the dusty stair. For a time Graham sat half unconscious. The journey from Chapelarroch had told on his not too hardy frame. The peril of his own life, and the thought of his wife and family, nearly drove him to distraction. Reviving a little from his gloomy condition, he rose and looked at the narrow window. The moon had just burst through a shattered cloud, revealing the hidden glories of the Highland loch, and Graham gazed rapturously on the scene. Around him was water, only water; beyond, in proud pre-eminence, rose the grand old Highland hills, the mist lying on their sides, with here and there the bald scalp of a rock peering through the silken covering, like islands in a sea. In the distance was heard the cry of the startled sea-gull, as the plunge of the prowling otter had scared it from its nest. Ever and anon came from the glens the hoarse calls of the parents of the flock, as the wild cat dashed on some unoffending lamb. On a corner of the old "keep" the barn-owl sat and watched, while the bats played around the walls. Below him, on the grass, sat the two sentries, muttering their Highland dirges, and chanting their war songs; and he could hear them whispering curses on the Sassenach for keeping them out of their heathery beds. Retiring from the window, Graham flung himself down on some heather in the corner of the room, and passed the night in sleep and reflection. Early in the following morning, Rob ordered the chamberlain to be brought into his presence. Rob, however, only taunted him about his present position, mingled with threats, and again ordered him back to his room. This continued from day to day for about three weeks, after which Rob Roy allowed him to return home. Before sending him away, however, he addressed him thus, " Now, chamberlain, if I had done what your usage of my family demanded in return, I should have hung you up by the neck; but, as Rob Roy never avenges himself on defenceless men, I allow you to return home. Remember, however, that the soil north of the Kelty is ours. The Macgregors lost it by unfair and cruel persecution, and by a gross breach of the right of succeeding generations; but so long as Rob Roy Macgregor lives, and his clan breathes in these glens, he shall not cease to take care of the rents himself. And you may tell your false master that, so long as he holds these lands, I shall continue to be his open enemy—and not of him alone, but of all who dare to seize the sacred soil of my fathers. For years my poor clansmen have been hunted, shot, and murdered; but remember, there is one head in Glengyle, and swords in Strathfillan, and God shall defend the right!" After the very merciful treatment which Graham had thus received, Montrose, partly in consideration of the leniency shown to his factor, and on account of the unjust treatment which Rob had been subjected to at his own hands, in a great measure ceased to persecute Rob. Macgregor, in turn, ceased to annoy Montrose, and for many years before his death Rob had given up all raids into the country of his old enemy.

LAST MOMENTS OF ROB ROY.

ROB ROY MACGREGOR died on the farm of Inverloch-larabeg, among the braes of Balquhidder, in 1735. When confined to bed, nearly worn out by the laborious vicissitudes of a long and restless life, and approaching dissolution stealing fast upon him, there occurred a scene which was singularly characteristic of the man. A person with whom he had had a quarrel called to see him; and on being made aware of this, Rob called to his attendants, "Raise me up; dress me in my best clothes; tie on my arms; place me in the great chair! That fellow shall never see me on a death-bed." His attendants instantly complied, and he received his visitor with cold civility. Before they parted the priest arrived, and conjured Rob, as he expected forgiveness from God, to bring his mind in his last moments to forgive all his enemies. Rob at first de- murred to this expostulation; and the priest, to enforce it, quoted part of the Lord's prayer. On hearing this, Rob said, "Ay, now, ye ha'e gi'en me baith law and gospel for't. It's a hard law; but I ken it's gospel." Then, turning to Rob Oig (young Rob), his son, he addressed him thus—"My sword and dirk lie there. Never draw them without reason, nor put them up without honour. I forgive my enemies; but see you to them, or may"——and he expired. Rob Roy lies in the church-yard of Balquhidder, beneath a plain stone, on the top of which is carved the outline of a sword, an appropriate emblem of the man and the times—

"Clan Alpine's omen, and her aid."

In surveying the character of Rob Roy Macgregor, many excellent traits appear, from which we cannot withhold our admiration. There are no doubt some incidents in his extraordinary career. which deserve reprehension; but when we consider the time in which he lived—a time when the whole northern parts of the kingdom were torn by civil discord, and distracted by politics—the Government having neither strength nor wisdom to arrest the evils that flowed from feudal chieftainship, we cease to wonder at the deeds he performed, or the liberties he took. Rob Roy was among the last of the true Highland chiefs of the old stock, who gloried in supporting the ancient dignity and independence of his race. For a long series of years his clan had been subjected to the most fearful and cruel persecution at the hands of Government and the more powerful neighbouring chiefs; and it seemed as if Rob had been raised up by Providence to retrieve the fallen fortunes of his clan, and to arrest the bloodshed of his kindred. Rob Roy had five sons, viz., Coll, James, Ronald, Duncan, and Robert. Of Coll there is very little known; he is, however, said to have been of a quiet and gentlemanly demeanour, and, according to the rev. editor of the "History of Stirlingshire," to have possessed "every manly virtue." James is said to have been of great stature, and generally known

as "James Mor" or "Big Jamie." He possessed largely
the fiery dash of the original Highlander; inherited,
to a very considerable extent, the military ardour of his
father; and was a stanch supporter of the ill-fated house of
Stuart. In 1745, James, along with his cousin, Macgregor
of Glengyle, and twelve of his men, took the fort of Inversnaid, and made eighty-nine of the soldiers prisoners.
He held the rank of Major under Prince Charles, and
commanded six companies of Macgregors at the battle of
Prestonpans, where he had the misfortune to get his thigh
bone broken. On account of this accident, he was unable
to follow his Prince in his ill-fated march into England;
but, on his return, he took an active part in the conclud-
ing battle of Culloden, where he again commanded several
companies of Macgregors. In the year 1752, James was
confined a prisoner in the Castle of Edinburgh, for the part
he took, along with his brother Robert, in the abduction of
Jean Keay; but effected his escape in the following extraordinary manner:—His daughter, who had come to Edinburgh,
conceived a most admirable plan for his escape. Having previously arranged her designs, she, on the evening of the 16th
November, 1752, dressed herself in the habit and character
of a cobbler, and, with a pair of old shoes in her hand, she
went to his prison. Her father instantly put on the disguise, and then commenced an angry dispute with the
supposed cobbler about an overcharge of the price, and
loud enough to be heard by the sentinels. Watching his
opportunity, he hurriedly left the room, and, under cover
of the darkness of night, managed to make his escape.
Being afraid to return to the Highlands, he took the road

to England, and, after severe and fatiguing travel, on the
evening of the fourth day after his escape, he found himself
benighted on a wild and lonely moor in Cumberland.
Travelling on through the darkness, he at length left the
moor and entered a large wood. Being unable to proceed
farther, he sat down at the foot of a tree, and bemoaned
his condition. Alone, far from home and all that were dear
to him, weary and hungry, he knew not what to do. The
thought of his wife and little ones at home almost broke
his heart; and the recollection of his own early and happy
days, spent among the green braes of his native Craigroystan, and the sunny banks of Loch-Lomond, harrowed his
soul. Happy would he have been, if, on the death of his
father, instead of fighting for "Prince Charlie," he had

> "Hung his weapons in the hall."

Now, hunted by the most gross persecution, and punished
for imaginary crimes to satisfy a weak but cruel and ill-
advised Government, his goods had become the prey of
envious and devouring neighbours. James had been but a
short time in the wood when he was suddenly aroused by
a wild halloo that echoed far through the dark forest,
followed by the sound of several voices. Taking this for
his pursuers, he started to his feet, clutched his dagger,
cocked the pistols his faithful daughter had folded in the
cobbler's apron, and swore to himself that he would die
rather than be taken. Listening for a little, the voices
began to grow faint, and he saw at a short distance the
glimmering of a light. Anxious to know who these night
marauders were, and what might be their errand, he crept

cautiously up to the light, and beheld an old woman holding a torch to three men, who were loading panniers on
their horses' backs.   Fancy his surprise to hear one of the
men speak in the broken accents of his own native Loch-
Katrine! and, standing beside the old woman with the
torch, he imagined he saw the form of old Billy Marshall,
the tinker, whom he often had befriended in Glengyle!
After the horsemen had ridden off, Macgregor stepped
up to the hut, and, tapping at the door, it was opened
by Marshall himself.   Although in the poor disguise of
a cobbler, he instantly recognised James, and gave him
hearty welcome.   Marshall hoped James would at present
excuse the poverty of his abode, as it was only temporary,
until some ill-will he had gotten to himself in Galloway,
for burning a stack-yard, would blow over.   James was
kindly entertained by the tinker for two days; and on the
third he and his host set out on horseback for Whitehaven,
where he got a fisherman's boat for the Isle of Man.
From thence he went to Ireland, where he sailed for
France.   James died in France, poverty-stricken and
broken-hearted, in October 1754; and with him passed
away one of his clan's most able and enthusiastic sup-
porters.

We might follow the chequered career of the sons of
Rob Roy through a long list of varied adventures and
trials, but as none of these are closely connected with the
locality, we shall confine ourselves to a few of the daring
exploits of "Young Rob," as he was called, as they are
of strong local interest, and eventually cost him his life.
Young Rob was the youngest son of Rob Roy, and said

to be only seventeen years of age at his father's death. Scarcely had his father been dead than he began his adventures by shooting his cousin, and ended his days on the scaffold. · Young Rob is said to have been tall, but of slender build, and he inherited to a considerable degree his father's dexterity at the sword. He appears to have been reckless and easily advised—the tool of his more cautious brothers, and, if taunted, would face a multitude single-handed; but was altogether sadly wanting in the great moral sagacity that distinguished his father, and that took him out of so many difficulties. That the sons of Rob Roy were sadly persecuted, there remains not a shadow of a doubt; that they committed excesses there can be no denial; but the fate of James and Robert was peculiarly severe. After the alleged murder of his cousin, Robert fled to France, and was present at the battle of Fontenoy, in Flanders, on 11th May 1745; and after his return he never was brought to trial for the supposed crime, and it was only for his part in the abduction of Jean Keay that he was brought to the scaffold. The evidence in that case being of the most conflicting kind, the rev. editor of the " History of Stirlingshire" says, Rob was executed " ostensibly on that score." As a proof of the manner in which these men were treated, I have only to mention one instance. James and Ronald were tried at Perth for their share in the murder of their cousin, but were declared " not guilty" by the jury; the judge, however, bound them over to keep the peace for seven years, under a penalty of two hundred pounds.

CHAPTER IN THE LIFE OF YOUNG ROB ROY.

IT was one evening in the month of June of the year 1750; the sun had sunk to rest behind the giant form of Ben-Lomond, and its golden rays had ceased to be visible on the neighbouring hill-tops; the mist lay close on the marsh; the shallop lay at anchor; the moorcock nestled deep among the heather; and the last echoes of the cuckoo had ceased to linger in the glens; while on the hills, the sheep lay close on the faulds, and the lambs were huddled together on the bracken knowes; the peasant had retired to sweet repose, and the " wag on the wa' " of the lone Highland cottage on the banks of the lake, had just tolled the dark hour of twelve; there was no breeze on the hill, and the loch lay unruffled; the mountain rill gurgled down the glen of Portend, while the souch of the waterfall in the pool of Glenny, mingled with the cry of the nightjar, only disturbed the quietude of the scene; the innkeeper at the Port— little, old, and grey—had just turned the old key in the rusty lock, drawn the big bar across the door, and resigned himself to sleep, when the trampling of feet and the sound of voices were heard. · "What is this?" muttered the old man to himself; " the cavalry back again!" and, starting to his feet, he hurried to the window, and was surprised to see a company of Highlandmen standing in front of the house,

the hilts of their swords glittering in the pale moonlight.
" Ah! the Macgregors on some black-mail excursion, I guess,"
thought the innkeeper; and presently he beheld the leader
of the gang, a tall handsome young Highlander, approach
the door and demand admittance. The summons was instantly obeyed; and recognising the speaker, the innkeeper
exclaimed, " O! Bob Oig* Macgregor!" " Well, Ure, how
goes it?" exclaimed Rob, as he pushed past the old man
into the house, followed by his gang. " Just keep quiet,
Highlandmen," replied Ure; and, re-barring the door, he
whispered into Rob's ear, " Have you seen the cavalry?"
Rob looked serious and answered, " No, we have not; have
they been here of late?" " They have been here all day,"
replied the innkeeper. " I suppose they are still stationed
at Cardross?" inquired Macgregor. " They are," answered
Ure; " but they have gone on to the Endrick for a day or
two, and are to be stationed at Balakinrain." " At Balakinrain!" repeated Rob; and he gazed at his men, while
their eyes rolled back on the speaker. " Curses on their
Sassenach heads!" said Rob; " if I had them on the heath
they should not annoy me so," and the angry clansman
stamped on the floor and adjusted his kilt.

" But," addressing Ure, " bring us something to eat and
drink; it's a stiff hill that of yours." " It is," replied Ure;
" but many a good horse and cow your father has driven
o'er Glenny." " Yes," continued Macgregor; " and I ex-
pect his son will ride another one o'er the Tyepers† before
the sun rise." " I'll tak a groat on that," replied the inn-

---

* Young Rob Roy Macgregor.

† A well-known track in the hill above the Lake.

keeper, as he laid down the bread and cheese; and, turning to Rob, whispered in his ear, "There's no as much of
the Macgregor in ye." Rob swore, and quaffed a horn of
whisky, while the old man laughed. "I guess the lads on
the Endrick will know we are Macgregors before this time
to-morrow," answered Rob, his cheek beginning to colour.
"Ah, I see," cried the innkeeper; "you're for off with
Napier's hunter." "I am," cried Rob exultingly. "Then,"
continued the innkeeper, "tak a friend's advice, and stay
on the north side of Forth; there's a trifle of your sort
below the heather on Balgair Moor already."* "Curse the
fellow!" roared Rob; and springing to his feet, he clutched
his sword exclaiming,

> " Am I afraid to scour the glen,
> Or yet to meet Strath-Endrick men ?
> I'm ready now to strike that band;
> I'll go and fetch her single-hand.
> That sword shall never see its sheath
> Until I house her in Monteith.
> I swear it now, and have it sworn—
> You'll see her at the Port the morn
> To-morrow shall that vow fulfil, ∙
> I'll land her safe beyond that hill !
> Macgregor ne'er shall foul his name,
> Nor cowardice e'er stain his fame—
> To-morrow I shall have the prize,
> Or Macgregor in Strath-Endrick lies."
> " Ha, ha ! man, Rob !" cried the taunting host,
> " We mind not for such empty boast;
> But gie's a pinch, send round the horn,†
> Ye'll maybe no come back the morn "

* This referred to the time when the Macgregors were defeated on the moor of
Balgair, by " Big Jock" and a company of Dun's.

† This massive relic, being a huge ram's horn, is the property of Mr. H. Graham,
Gateside, Port; but is at present in Glasgow.

Rob quick the rustic horn did pass,
And helped himself to flowing glass
But quick as they did quaff their wine,
As fast did roll unheeded time;
Hour after hour did onward flee,
Until the rustic clock struck three.
Macgregor started from his seat,
And soon the band were on their feet.
His favourite sword did catch his eye,
Before him, as 't did naked lie;
He'd ne'er forgot what passed before,
But now did mind the oath he swore.
He seemed as if in solemn mood—
His kinsmen round in silence stood,
And well each single eye could trace
The cloud upon the chieftain's face.
The brow upon that manly form
Lower'd like the cloud in coming storm,
Which told his mind, and showed his will—
Fierce as the blast that sweeps yon hill.
His heaving breast told but in part
What wild emotions filled his heart.
The former taunts had still their pang,
Deep through his soul their echoes rang—
Rung at his nerves, till hope and pride
Dashed, like a thought, them all aside.
The crowing cock, out in the lawn,
Told Rob that early day did dawn;
The chirping bird, amid the thorn,
With joy did hail the approaching morn:
Ben-Lomond, still though in a cloud,
Did fast throw off the nightly shroud;
The rising mist from off the hill
Showed the curling smoke from smuggler's still;
The smiling lake, like silver grey—
The shallop on its bosom lay;
The tawny owl no more did roam,
But sought her nest in Inchmahome;
The herons screeched amid the brake;
Sea-gulls flaunted o'er the lake;
The scared duck, or wild drake's quack,
Was heard at distant Arnmauk;

The cunning fox, that out had stole,
Was seen returning to its hole;
Each drooping flower anew was born,—
The rising sun pronounced the morn!
Along the shore Rob fast did glide,
With stately step and manly stride;
He never tired, nor stopped to rest,
His fate still struggling in his breast.
He mused hard on his mad crusade,
But he trusted in his arm and blade;
He'd pledged his word, likewise his name—
He'd rather die than stain his fame.
Before the clock had counted ten,
Rob was seen at Balakinrain.
There, in a field before his gaze,
The coveted steed at large did graze.
He seized her soon, and o'er her strode—
Like falcon's swoop, he's on the road.
The soldiers to their horses flew,
And after him with wild halloo.
Quick sped the flight—on went the race—
More glorious far than hunter's chase!
Like drifting cloud before the gale,
The chieftain sweeps along the vale.
Quick in his course he on did dash,
And cross'd the moor like lightning's flash.
When he Buchlyvie village near,
They full a mile are in the rear;
On he swept through fair Garden,
And faster still he headed them.
The noise re-echoed up the glen,
As they sped on through field and fen.
The traveller paused, and mused in wonder—
The trampling seemed like distant thunder;
The peasant ceased awhile his toil,
And wondered at the great turmoil.
The startled hare did flee her den;
The frighted roe took 'cross the plain,
The heron started from the fern;
The cunning fox kept close his cairn—
Retiring, 'mid the thicket fast,
He viewed the storm go sweeping past.

Rob soon did reach the river Forth,
Which bounds the south lands from the north,
He reached it, and, with a stride,
He landed on the distant side.
They, too, did reach the Forth, I ween,
But man and horse plunged in the stream
Down they sank beneath the surge;
But soon again were on the verge—
Some weaponless, and some half-drowned,—
Exhausted horse lay on the ground.
They were all safe, but thanks to Heaven
That none to death, or worse, were driven!
Their leader cried, "Why will ye halt?
Ho! horsemen, in your saddles vault!
The robber's gone across the heath,
And to the hills of wild Monteith!"
Fast as thought they were astride,
And onward dashed the madd'ning ride *
Cardross fields they had swept through,
When Glenny hill burst on their view;
But deeming that he could not pass
Yon rugged hill which guards the pass,
Still on he goes at lightning speed.
No slacking seeks the noble steed:
Dykes and ditches, too, he meets—
O'er all the gallant courser sweeps.
He soon did reach the mountain base,
And for a moment stopped to gaze;
Around he for a second glanced,
And viewed them as they onward pranced.

Rob now began, for safety's sake,
To think what's best the course to take.
He fain would go to Aberfoyle,
But the panting steed can't face such toil,
Her trembling limbs full well he feels,
And death comes thundering at his heels.

* Information from the late Alexander Dun of Kepdowrie, who had it from his uncle, John Dun of Kepdowrie, who was present on the road leading to the Port, and saw Rob ride past, pursued by the dragoons. The animal on which Rob rode, said to be a " grey mare," was without saddle or bridle, while the Dragoons were full mounted.

Longer there he cannot bide;
Destruction waits on every side;
Before him towers the rugged steep,
Behind, the lake lies dark and deep,
Onward, pursuers press him throng,
As raging torrents dash along;
More desperate they than yet they seem—
Bright in the sun their lances gleam.
The chieftain at the steep they view,
Each horseman feels his strength renew;
And hope begins to fire each vein,
That they would yet the steed regain.
But Rob ere this matured his plan,
And with a glance the hill did scan;
He firmly then the reins did clasp,
And seized the mane with giant grasp;
He quickly then his rowels plied,
And plunged them in the horse's side.
Like arrow shot from out the bow,
The daring horseman on did go—
Like dust before the western breeze,
Quick he vanished 'mong the trees,—
Like wild roe, far from hunter's ken,
Up dashed Macgregor through the glen,
And safely there his prize did hide
On rugged Glenny's northern side.

FROM STIRLING TO INCHMAHOME.

THE clock had tolled the death-knell of April; the last echoes of Spring had just been thundered from the steeple clock, and had died away amid the dark recesses of the town; it was still; naught was heard save the tread of the lonely sentinel, or the wail of the tawny owl as it floated around the Castle rock; the night watchman at the station, with muffled form and lamp in hand, had just signalled the last train of the night, and as it dashed through the gloom, snorting like some mighty steed, with a tread like the roar of thunder and eyes of flame, you heard its shrill scream, like the cry of the wild eagle, sending its echoes far among the Castle rocks, till the Abbey Craig whispered back the sound. We mused on the past, and smilingly looked on toward the future. We had made up our minds for a week at the Port, and although not in actual possession, still in a great measure we were enjoying the beautiful reality. In fancy we were climbing the hill, rambling through its ferny glens, or catching the finny tribe in the silvery waters of the lake. Early on the morning of the 1st May, we could be seen, basket on back and fishing-rod in hand, pacing the platform of Stirling station, anxiously awaiting the ringing of the last bell. " Long looked for comes at last:" no sooner had the last bell given its first

tinkle, than my companion plunged into a first-class carriage—I, of course, following hard at his heels—placing
ourselves under the care of "old Hugh." All now seems
bustle and animation—porters running with luggage, passengers taking their seats, while the bang of the carriage-doors
lends music to the scene. Suddenly the short "All right!"
sounds in our ears, a sharp, shrill whistle is heard in front,
while the clankling of the couplings tells us we are on the
road; and in the twinkling of an eye we are sweeping
round the Castle rock and entering the rich Carse of Stirling. As we roll past, we look on the old grey face of the
Castle, and think of the changes—the fetes and the fights
that have ever and anon been enacted on its summit, since
the Roman Eagle first spread her wings on its bald head!
Onwards dashes the locomotive; and as we look out of
the carriage window, we can see the smoky spires of
Stirling fast dying in the distance. On our right rolls the
sluggish Forth; and Craigforth, that proud usurper of the
Pass, rears its head in the morning sunshine. On our
left stretches the dark hills of Touch and Boquhan; and
as our eyes scan their rocky face, we see the falcon hunting
after his morning meal. Approaching Kippen, we get a
glimpse of the famous glen of Boquhan—famous in traditional and historic lore, and

> "Where to the skies
> The riven rocks fantastic rise."

By-and-by, we reach the Port of Monteith station, and
instantly we are out on the platform. The train disappears, and we hear its hollow sound dying in the distance,
like the echoes of distant thunder. We are now left to

ourselves; and we look around us on the prettiest of all country stations. We gaze on the flowers and the green fields, with the dark blue hills beyond,

"Lending enchantment to the view."

The dark green woods at our side are loud with the din of birds, as they pour forth their morning songs of praise. Happy native!—let him "bless his stars." Away from the din and turmoil of the city, he roams a free subject of the woods and fields! Here nothing disturbs the quiet serenity of Nature, save the thundering of the "iron horse," or the wild whistle of the locomotive. We pass on our way to the Port, where the road is beautiful and every foot is classic. Half-a-mile from the station we pass the old bridge of Cardross, famous in prophecy and tradition. Near to it is the place where Rob Roy crossed the Forth with his stolen steed, when pursued by a troop of dragoons. Near to it, also, in days of yore, stood the "Ferry Inns," in which Prince Charles Stuart refreshed himself, or, as some say, slept a night, when on a visit to Buchanan of Arnprior. Near to it, also, is the gentle flowing spring of the once far-famed "Gout Well of Cardross." On the left hand side of the road there is a considerable knoll, from the top of which we have a beautiful view of the surrounding country. We see the Forth roll on in queenly pride, while on her downy banks graze the sober cattle. We pass the Lodge of Cardross, and, farther on, the hamlet of Dykehead, which boasts of a school, a smithy, and wright's shop. Children are playing at the school-door, the joiner grating away at his bench, while the clank of the smith's hammer lends a chorus to the rustic scene. The road in front of us is beautifully shaded with stately oaks, skirted on the right by the well-kept grounds of Cardross. On our left is a dark forest, some miles in length; and we can see the simple roe bounding for protection far amid its dark recesses. Here we get a beautiful glimpse of the Hill of Glenny, its top rising high above the trees, as if it threatened to stop our northward passage. We now reach the seques-tered and romantic cottage of Tomavhoid (or Courthill), where, in days long gone by, the neighbouring lairds sat in final judgment on the offending wretches of their estates. We look around, and our eye rests on a hoary ash, sending its grey branches wide to the breeze, whose old boughs served the purpose of our new-fashioned scaffolds, when the rustic native of the cottage performed the part of modern Calcraft. Our thoughts wander back some hundred years; imagination paints the assembled throng,—the proud laird, with sullen and merciless face, wielding the sceptre of his relentless feudal power—the pitying looks of his attend-ants, as they turn their eyes to gaze upon the fellow-mortal on his way to the drop;—ay, methinks I see the poor culprit, as he kicks high and dry upon the branch! But why fatigue the imagination with scenes like these? Feudal days are past, the court has vanished, and the mark of the rope has disappeared.

Leaving Tomavhoid, we have a beautiful, varied, and interesting view of the Lake of Monteith and surrounding country. To the left we get a fine prospect of the west Grampians—Ben-Lomond keeping watch and ward over nether land, with an outstretching plain of cultivated fields,

dark forest, and barren moor between. In front are the
green knolls of Inchie—the lake and the blooming heath-
clad hills of Monteith beyond. On our right are the
mansions of Rednock and Blairhoyle, embosomed among
fine old trees are the famous Moss of Flanders. Around it
the historic Gudie rolls smoothly along. Beyond are the
sunny braes of Ruskie, with the dark outline of the Ochils
in the distance. Passing Inchie House, the scene deepens,
and the sight becomes charming. The lake, with all its
loveliness, bursts upon our view. On the south side of
the lake we get a glimpse of Lochen House, surrounded
by stately trees—the pleasure-grounds skirting the water.
Farther on, we see the romantic Arnmauk covered with
her dark waving pines, and stretching her long arm far
into the deep;—attempting to shake hands with the isle.
In the background we see the mansion of Gartmore, with
the dark fir hill beyond. Farther north, we see the rugged
pass and scattered crags of Aberfoyle. We pass on; our
eye dazzles with the beauty of the landscape, our mind is
pleased with the calm grandeur of the scene, our soul is
filled with instruction, and we are anxious to get to the
hotel. And as we walk along the lake's pebbled shore,
and gaze upwards, onwards, and around, beauty skirts us on
either side. On our right are the wooded slopes of Rednock, where the creeping fern entwines itself with the green
moss, and the "blue bells of Scotland" fill the air with
their fragrance. On our left lies the silvery waters of the
lake, with Inchmahome resting on its bosom, and the blue
heavens and grey towering clouds mirrored in its glossy
surface. The sea-gull skims along its bosom; the wild

swan spreads her wings to catch the floating zephyr; while the cormorant feeds among the reeds. We see the osprey, as the noble bird soars above the waters, eyeing some sportive pike, and pinioned in mid air, as if transfixed between the heavens and the earth; then, with a swoop like a flash of lightning, he disappears below the blue waters, and again, with triumphant scream, soars away with the finny prey to his mate on yonder rock. Before us stands the church, the mausoleum of the house of Gartmore, and the grave-yard, where the native dust in peace reposes. The beautifully situated hotel; the neat manse, ensconsed among trees; behind, the hill of Glenny, bursting high up suddenly from the plain, where, like some aged sire with wrinkled face and bald head, he stands,

"The guardian angel of the lake."

The dark firs that clothe its front contrast beautifully with the brown heath upon its summit. We enter the hotel; lounge on the sofa, puff our Havannah, sip our sherry, and order a boat to convey us to the island. We are taking a last whiff, and giving orders for dinner, when the door gently opens, and an old Celt, doffing his bonnet, politely informs us that he is waiting to row us to Inchmahome. We gaze upon the form before us; we mark his grey hairs and weather-beaten brow, brown as the heath on his native Mondhuie. My companion mutters " Can this be the boatman?" We are almost afraid to place ourselves under his care, or risk a voyage in his tiny barge. But as he walks before us to the shore, we see something in his gait and manner which convinces us that he is no ordinary

boatman; and, with feelings of confidence, we take our seats
by his side, and soon find that we are under the charge
of a true son of the Græme,* and that the spirit of that
ancient clan fills the old man's bosom, while its blood flows
pure in his veins. We have just been seated, when we
find his memory fresh with all the legendary tales and
fairy incidents of his cherished vale, while he is deep
read in historic lore; and as, with clutched oar and bent
back, the eager old man pulls on through the blue waters,
he points us to the pass, where, in days gone by, their
native Glenny vomited forth her warrior sons on the red
hosts of Cromwell, and, like the mighty avalanche from
the brow of yonder hill, crushed the invaders. He points
us also to Portend's craggy glen, where, rock built on rock,
it raises its riven head far in mid air, and, with ragged face,
shattered brow, and tottering form, stands

"Nodding o'er the cavern grey."

He tells you of its deep pools and tumbling waterfalls, and
of the rare ferns that clothe its banks and adorn its sides.
Behind we see Bendhu, with blue head and barren face,
its bare rocks glancing in the summer sun. On the lake's
reedy margin we see the feathered steep of the Cowden,
through the shadows of the noble oaks that clothe its side,
deep in the blue waters. But ere we have half surveyed
the grandeur of hill and glen, our boat strikes the landing-
place, and we turn to gaze on the varied glories of Inch-

* The venerable Mr Hugh Graham, Gateside, Port of Monteith, the respected
representative of the ancient Grahams of Mondhuie, and to whom the author is
highly indebted for the tradition of the "Earl's Niece," &c Parties visiting the Lake
should call on Mr. Graham, and they will find he can "preach without a paper."

mahome, as they loom before us in the huge and hoary wreck that stands with skeleton form, the monument of the zeal of our early fathers; or in the noble trees that shoot their giant antlers high in the breeze. We spend the afternoon among the sacred relics of the Priory and Queen's Garden, and then return to spend the night at the inn.

We are astir early in the morning; we find the weather, as it always is at the Lake of Monteith, clear and beautiful; and as we look out of our bed-room window, we gaze on a landscape of placid beauty, the fairest our eye has ever beheld—a landscape famous in history, poetry, and romance. Before us stand the grand old Highland hills, ·their tops clear, but the grey mist crawling along their boggy sides, here and there tinged with the golden rays of the summer sun, and throwing a few dark shadows deep into the·waters. We see the lake in all its loveliness, with the ruins of Inchmahome looking through the hoary branches that adorn the isle—the isle which kings and queens delighted to honour with their presence—the isle, once the birth-place of earls, the home of royalty, the favourite resort of monarchs, the safe retreat of queens. A shallop, with oars ready, lies beneath our window, and we see the sea-fowl playing over the blue waters. The hill and the lake are alike tempting, and we now begin to discuss whether we shall storm the hill, or launch out on the lake and enjoy the glorious sensation of hooking some greedy pike, or inhale the mountain's balmy breeze. We soon decide. To-day, the hill is clear and robed in sunshine; to-morrow, that rampart of Nature may be wrapped in its misty mantle, and the golden tints of to-day be chased away by to-morrow's sweeping blast. We discuss breakfast; fill our flasks with "the real naked truth," as our kind hostess termed it, and which, I dare say, might have the advantage of " never seeing a gauger;" and soon we are marching up the hill. Before us stands the place where Rob Roy, one hundred years ago, dashed up the hill with his foaming steed, while being pursued by a troop of English dragoons. We ascend the knoll on which it is said he stopped to rest the noble animal, and gaze back on his pursuers, as they swept round the lake like a whirlwind, and came on like a rolling flood. We fancy we see the outlawed chief making preparations for the final effort. As the eagle, high on yon dizzy cliff, plants his wings before making the final dart upon his victim, Macgregor plants his knees and his rowels firm into his horse's sides, and, with a few terrific plunges, each like the swoop of the falcon, the hero chief vanishes over the summit. We hurry on up the rugged slope of Glenny, where,

> " With crown of heath and brow of stone,
> Crockmelly rears her head alone;
> And watching o'er the inlet brake,
> The guardian angel of the lake "

The hill is already fresh with the glories of summer, and as we ascend its fern-covered sides, and climb its breckan braes, we breathe the heather gale, and inhale the fresh mountain breeze, balmy as it ever floats around Monteith, and see the creeping moss clinging to the jutting rocks. By-and-by we reach the summit, and after taking " a refresher," we gaze downwards and onwards. A scene intensely interesting meets our view. We will not compare it with the bold sweep, as seen from the towering top of

Ben-Nevis, or the gorgeous display of Highland grandeur as witnessed from the princely summit of Ben-Lomond, but for variety of Highland and Lowland scenery, heathy hill and wooded dale, lowland lake and mountain stream, is unsurpassed by any of the lesser hills in Scotland. Around you, on either side, behind and before, lie the scattered glories of Monteith. In front you look down on the valley of the Græme, behind we gaze far back on the country of the Macgregor. To the south we see what was once an ice-bound ocean, now a lovely valley, watered with rivers, adorned with lakes, studded with trees, dotted with mansions, beautified with glens, clothed with their native ferns, hushed to slumber mid the din of waterfalls. Before us lies the Lake of Monteith, with its three isolated islands resting on its bosom like specks on a vast mirror; the quiet country highway winds along the shore, like a huge native adder in its coil, cooling its poisoned tongue in the silvery rivers. To the east we scan a long and wide tree-shaded country. Our eye ranges the carse of Stirling, and rests on the Castle rock, while far beyond we trace the dark outlines of Edinburgh Castle mingling with the distant sky. To the west we see Aberfoyle's classic hills and glens. To the north we gaze far back on the country of Clan-Alpine—a country famous for the deeds of its sons, and the glories of its scenery—a country famous for the exploits of kings, the home of Rob Roy, the birth-place of Roderick Dhu. We look around us, and at once fourteen Highland lakes burst upon our awe-struck view. Many of those mountain tarns repose amid the seclusion of their native hills, so sheltered by the heathy mountains, that the hurricanes of

I

winter never disturb, nor the zephyrs of summer kiss their
waters.   Before us on the north lie Lochs Vennacher and
Achray, the road from Callander to the Trossachs winding
along the shore, while the huge form of Ben-Ledi towers
beyond.   We see the wood-adorned summits of the Trossachs, Loch-Katrine up among the hills, with Glengyle
and the misty tops of Balquhidder in the background.
As we look around on the Highland country, and admire
the glories of the Creator's works, as they stand before us
in the grey mountain, sink deep in the rugged glen,
stretch out in the green valley, or dip amid the placid
waters, our mind wanders back to the marauding character of its inhabitants, when the hardy natives of the hills
and glens learned only to handle the bow and studied
nothing but the sword; and oft has the heath on this
mountain side been dyed by the blood of those who
fell in the fierce conflicts between the Macgregors and
the Grahams, in the days of the war cry and fiery cross.
Those days are now gone, and as we look around on the
peaceful scene, we think of the change since the wild boar
roamed through its marshes, and the wolf growled deep in
its caverns—since the wild cry of the war-chief was heard
from the hill, or saw him return with his trophies.   There
was a time, and that not long ago, when the blood-hound
tore the Macgregor, and the eagle fed on his carcase.   Ay,
we fancy we can see the blood-bespattered beast, as he
returns from his fell mission, snuffing the fresh breeze or
lapping his gory fangs; or hearken to the mountain raven, as
he perches on, and picks the eyes out of the fallen victim,
when that brave but ill-used and unhappy clan was hunted

like foxes among their covers, and stalked like deers on their loved native hills. But those scenes have passed away. The cottagers of the glens and the natives of the hill-sides alike dwell in security—their sons are trained to industry, and their daughters spring up like mountain daisies, born to blush unseen. The howl of the blood-hound gives place to the bleating of the lamb; and the voice of the war-chief finds an echo in the herdman's pipe, or the song of the shepherd's daughter. True, the flocks may yet be startled by the inroads of the fox or the cry of the black eagle, as the king of birds sweeps over the grey mountain, away to his home among the dizzy cliffs.

DOING ABERFOYLE—BY A GLASGOW TOURIST.*

LOOKING out for a new route is the " look out" of every
tourist who has been regularly "doing" the Highlands,
season after season, as the writer has done for some years;
and as each successive summer rolls past, the difficulty
becomes more and more great of finding some new and
interesting district of country, alike interesting to the
invalid, the tourist, the geologist, and antiquarian.   Permit
me, then, Mr. Editor, to inform my brother tourists that
such a route has, by the kind liberality of one of the most
liberal hotel proprietors in Scotland, just been opened to
the public, and almost by mere accident.   I, one day at
the end of last week, had the unbounded pleasure of being
driven through it at "Jehu" speed.   Having seen, in one
of the Forth & Clyde Railway time-tables, that I could
leave the City at 9.35 a.m., reach Port of Monteith station
at 11.20, and "do" the Lake of Monteith, Aberfoyle, Loch-
Ard, Loch-Chon, Inversnaid, and Loch-Lomond, returning
to Glasgow at 8 p.m., and all for " sixteen bob," it struck
me as something " decidedly new."   Determined to make
a trial of the new route, on the morning of Saturday last I
found myself at Port of Monteith station, exactly at 11.20;

* Written for the *Glasgow Herald*, July, 1865. This route is not open beyond
the Lake of Monteith this season, 1866.

and after surveying the prettiest of all country stations, I, along with a few other passengers, mounted the coach and took my seat beside "Willie," as I heard some of the railway officials term the driver. We were scarcely seated, when onwards plunged the noble steeds, at a rate little short of "the limited mail;" and I had not proceeded far when I found our driver the most civil and agreeable companion I had ever sat beside. Being a native of the district, his mind was well stored with the traditions of the country, and rich in historic lore. About half a mile from the station you cross the Forth, when he points you to the place where the great Rob Roy crossed the river with his prize when on a horse-stealing excursion in Strath-Endrick. He also points you to the place where, in days gone by, there stood the "Ferry Inns," in which the young Pretender slept a night when visiting his friends in Monteith. Near this also flowed the spring once so famous for curing the gout. The road in front of you is beautifully shaded; on the right are the well-kept grounds of Cardross, and on your left dark green forests some miles in length, where you may see the roe bounding far ben among its dark recesses. On your right stands a sequestered little cottage, with a row of large trees at the back; and Willie tells you that is the old "hanging hill" of Cardross; while he points you to a hoary ash, whose boughs used to serve the purpose of our new-fashioned scaffold, when the rustic native of the hut acted the part of our modern Calcraft. He now tells you to look before you, and a scene the most dazzling your eyes ever beheld bursts upon your view. One glance of your eye, and you scan forest, field, lake, and mountain, all fresh with the glories

of summer, spread out before you. As you sweep past
the green knolls of Inchie, and the road winds close to the
Lake of Monteith, this charming sheet of water increases
in loveliness. The waters are smooth as glass, and clear
as the crystal stream, contrasting beautifully with the green
fairy islands that repose upon its bosom. Inchmahome,
the largest of the islands, contains the ruins of the earliest
Augustinian monastery in Scotland, the still existing ruins
bearing proof of its once ancient grandeur. This island
is also famous as the early burying-ground of the great
feudal chiefs of the district, and for having been some
time the residence of Mary, Queen of Scots; when she often
played with her "four Marys," and planted the "Boxwood
Bower," which still remains, bearing the name of the maiden
queen. As you sweep round the northern side of the
lake, you get a fine view of the historic hill of Glenny,
clothed with its green firs, contrasting beautifully with the
brown heath upon its summit. Willie here points you to
the place where Rob Roy galloped up the hill with his
stolen steed, and to the knoll where he halted to rest his
fleet prize, and gaze back on his pursuers as they swept
round the lake like a whirlwind, and came on like a rolling
flood. Here the "Grahams of Glenny" rushed down their
native passes, like avalanches from the mountain, on Cromwell's army in the year 1653. You are now rolling past the
most southern portion of the great Grampian range; and
Bendhu, with barren face and heath-covered head, rises on
your right. Here you are told to look back and take a
long last look of the placid loveliness of Monteith before
entering the stern glories of Aberfoyle; and as you pass

through its scattered crags, and defile among its shattered hills, you feel an awe-stirring sensation rising within you; but, ere you have time to think or reflect, Willie rattles up to the door of the far-famed " Bailie Nicol Jarvie." Here a pair of fresh horses are got, and during the unyoking process you have plenty of time to step into the inn and have your tumbler, where you will find everything of the best, with most prompt attendance. Leaving the inn, the scenery becomes more and more interesting. On your right rises Craigmore, with rugged face and bald head, the falcons floating round its summit, and the wrecks of a thousand ages at its base. At your feet, the Avondhu rolls over its rocky bed; and on your left lies the historic Duchray, with its grey castle and hoary strongholds, its " ivy mantled" turrets and dark dungeons, its rocky passes and ferny glens. After passing "the Clachan," at a high turn of the road, the finest sight of this intensely interesting locality is to be had. Loch-Ard opens beautifully to the view; you see the silvery waters of the loch dazzling in the noonday sun, and around its varied charms. You see its feathered banks and heath-capped knolls; its rising hills and deep gorges; with the frowning Ben-Lomond looking down on the scene below. As you roll on through woods and meadow lands, and emerge from the thick shades of the silver birches, the whole loch gradually opens to the view. Here Willie points you to Rob Roy's cave, where the great freebooter sometimes spent a night when hard pressed. Here there is a fine echo, and you can yet hear the gruff voice of the great native war chief issuing from the crags. Here also you will see the rock, the scene of the collision.

between the Macgregors and the redcoats; and you can fancy you hear the hysteric laugh of Helen Macgregor, as she gazes on the " bubbles " that dance on her victim's grave. Here also you are rolled under the roots of the tree that caught hold of the Bailie's riding coat, and dangled him between the heavens and the earth. Near the western shore of the loch you see Duke Murdoch's island, where tradition says he spent his last night on earth, having been taken from there to Stirling on the morning of his execution. On the north side of the loch, and near its upper extremity, is the famous waterfall of Ledard, noted by the great novelist in both " Rob Roy " and " Waverley." After this, for some distance, you find the road partaking considerably of the up-and-down style; but never mind that, Willie can rattle over it like Jehu of old; and as you near Loch-Chon, he points out to you Rob Roy's well, and near it a cattle-lifter's grave. You find Loch-Chon grander than Loch-Ard, but not so extensive or famous. Looking down from the top of the coach you fancy the loch to be some hundred feet below you, with several small islands resting on its still waters. The islands are the favourite resort of otters; and amid the crags of the high hills that tower beyond the native wild cat lingers still. Here you get a beautiful view of the top of Ben-Lomond opening wide its yawning jaws. You are now nearing the road from Inversnaid to Loch-Katrine, and you get a fine sight of the latter, with the surrounding hills and " the braes of Balquhidder" in the distance. You pass, on your left, the small loch, Arklet, on whose banks the fair heroine Helen Macgregor, the wife of Rob Roy, was born. Approaching Inversnaid, on your right, and on a commanding eminence, stands the remains of the once famous garrison of Inversnaid, erected by Government in the year 1713 to overawe the clan Gregor. Before you, in grand magnificence, rise the hills of Loch-Lomond, and on your left flow the dark waters of the Arklet over its wild and rugged bed, until it tumbles, amid wild grandeur, into the bosom of Loch-Lomond. You have now reached Inversnaid—you are in rare trim for dinner, and you find you have just as much time as perform that important operation before the steamer calls to take you on to Glasgow. At Inversnaid you find everything in the highest possible order; and to your kind and intelligent host you are indebted for the opening up of the Monteith and Aberfoyle route—a route which, for the grand variety of its scenery, "stands alone in its glory," and but for him it would have remained almost unseen and unknown.

CARDROSS—ITS MOSSES—THEIR AGE
AND TREASURE.

THE ancient and fine estate of Cardross is beautifully situated in the centre of that most charming of all charming districts, the district of Monteith. On either side lies stretched the luxuriant plains, teeming with Nature's glories, and hallowed by historical and traditional associations. Around it the hills rise, the glens dip deep, lakes repose, and rivers roll their dark waters. The serpentine Forth pursues its sluggish course for miles through and around its southern marches, the silvery waters of the Lake of Monteith, and the historic Goodie, wash its northern boundaries, while the heath-capped Grampians throw their shadows over it.

The historical and traditionary associations that linger around its ancient walls, where sage king sat and youthful queens frolicked; its noble park, with its grand old trees, spreading wide their hoary arms, and rearing high their antlered heads; its well-kept garden, clad with down and rose; and the waveless loch, where the swan with zephyr-ruffled wing floats proudly along, and the heron, springing from the reedy inlet, tend to make it, to the historian, the traditionist, and Nature's worshipper, one of the most interesting estates in the kingdom.

Cardross, in Gaelic, signifies "The Fort on the Promontory." It was originally a Roman station, and on each side of the mansion-house can yet be seen the old Roman pathway. During the great historic period, Cardross was the haunt of many of the greatest men in Scottish history. King Robert Bruce spent some time here, between the time of his coronation and the battle of Bannockburn; and one account says he slept in the house the night previous to his great victory. Some historians state also that the renowned king died here; but that event, I am inclined to think, happened at Cardross in Dumbartonshire. Bruce's sword is still carefully preserved in Cardross house, and this extraordinary weapon is traditionally stated to have been left by Bruce on one of his visits. Whether or not it belonged to the hero-king can never be correctly known, but there can be little doubt that it is a sword of the period. It measures over all 6 feet $2\frac{1}{2}$ inches, blade 4 feet $7\frac{1}{2}$ inches, breadth at hilt $2\frac{1}{2}$ inches, and weighs no less than 10 lbs.

George Buchanan, the great Scottish historian, spent his boyhood on the estate of Cardross. George's father having died in early life, the family was taken in charge by James Heriot, their maternal uncle, who leased two farms from the Earl of Mar for behoof of the widow and family. The lease, dated and signed, is still preserved among the Cardross papers. John, seventh Earl of Mar, along with James VI., was afterwards educated by George Buchanan. Rather curious that the King of Scotland and an earl's son should be educated by an orphan boy, the son of a tenant on Cardross estate! Queen Mary was a frequent visitor at the house, during the time she resided with her guardians on the island of Inchmahome.

Cardross was garrisoned by a detachment of Cromwell's army after the battle of Aberfoyle, in 1653; and here General Monk issued an order to the Earl of Monteith to cut down the woods of the Glashard, as they gave great protection to the royalists, and also to raise men to guard the passes of Monteith and Aberfoyle. He collected from his estate " forty-two " Grahams, who were known in the district as the " forty-twa," or " the black watch." The men were never disbanded, and this was the original foundation of the now distinguished " forty-second " regiment. The original order is still preserved among the Monteith papers at Gartmore house, and is signed George Monk.

The renowned Marquis of Montrose garrisoned Cardross for a short period, and an interesting original letter of his was discovered by the present proprietor, when searching for material for this article. " Prince Charlie," during the rebellion of 1745, and while on his route from the north to Stirling, called at what was then known as the " Ferry Inn," and partook of some refreshment. Near this was the once celebrated " Gout Well," the waters of which were famed for curing the gout. During the palmy days of this inn, the well was regularly visited by numbers of cripples who were affected with that disease; but whether the " impotent folk" drank of the well; or waited for the " moving of the waters," I have been unable to determine. One thing, however, seems certain, that after the present bridge was built, and the inn demolished, believers in its virtue became " small by degrees and beautifully less," and now the crystal spring gurgles over the primrose bank unheeded and unknown.

Cardross is also celebrated as being the traditional scene of the old "tragical ballad" of "Sir James the Rose" and "Matilda Erskine." The tragedy is supposed to have been enacted some short time after the battle of Flodden, and during the time the estate was held by the Buchan family.

About thirty years ago, when levelling the ground for an artificial flower garden, at the south-west corner of the mansion-house, a very considerable quantity of human bones were discovered, and only a very short space below the surface. Whether or not these were the remains of Matilda and her lovers, is now beyond being set at rest, but all things considered, they certainly give a strong colouring to the old and interesting tradition.

On Cardross estate lies a large tract of that remarkable deposit called "Flanders Moss," which extends from the village of Gartmore to a point opposite the village of Thornhill, embracing in extent some thousands of acres, and varying from five to twenty feet in depth. Graham of Duchray, writing in the year 1724, says the moss extended from the hill of Gartmore to "within two or three miles of Stirling, on both sides of the Forth." The persevering industry, however, of a century and a half since the laird of Duchray wrote, and the last fifty years of that period—fraught with all that science and modern ingenuity could invent—have told its wonders, as the beautiful and fertile Carse of Stirling now shows. On Cardross alone several hundred acres of the very finest land have been reclaimed,

now yielding to the landlord from one to two pounds
an acre, whereas his ancestors failed to realise as many
farthings.

The whole level tract of country extending from Stirling
to the heath-clad Lennox moors, was no doubt at one
period a large inland lake, and that lake the last declining
remnant of a great ice-bound sea, which has left its traces
in the grooved and smooth surface of the rocks of our hills
and lake shores. That this district of country was covered
with water, and navigable by the early inhabitants, is abundantly proved by the discoveries of the remains of ancient
canoes. Some time ago a very perfect specimen of a canoe
was discovered under the moss beneath the village of Gartmore; and in 1724 there was, at the Firhill of Gartmore,
a stone with a large ring in it—at that time called the
" Clachnan Loang," or the " Ship or Boat Stone"—and
traditionally said to have been used for the purpose of
boats or ships making fast.

The vulgar traditions regarding this moss, its name and
origin, are rather amusing. One of these is, that it floated
from Flanders, and hence the name; another is, that the
country originally paid taxes to Denmark for the use of
the moss, and it was only got quit of through the great
sagacity of George Buchanan, the historian, threatening the
authorities there, that if the tax was not cancelled the moss
would be immediately returned. Whether the great historian meant to do this by bringing on a "roarin', spate," I
have been unable to determine. Many and conflicting are
the theories propounded regarding the age, origin, and
composition of this moss. One sort of popular idea is, that

it is the wreck of ages, gathered by overflowing rivers, and washed down by storms from the hills and higher grounds, and lodged in the valleys beneath. My own opinion, however, is of a different character; and from a somewhat intimate knowledge of the district, borne out by minute inquiries of those who have spent long and laborious lives in clearing away the different mosses of the country, I have formed the following conclusions on the matter; but should any of my readers hold opposite views I shall be glad to hear them explained:—

Considering, then, that this level tract was originally an inland lake, after the gradual subsidence of the water the land would become partially drained, by the water sinking into natural ruts in the clay, and which in a great measure would pave the way for the great and rapid growth of heavy timber which appears to have immediately followed. This timber comprises oak, fir, birch, and hazel—chiefly the former as large wood, and the latter as underwood. On the farm of Parks, on the estate of Cardross, there seems to have been a considerable quantity of fir. Previous to the invasion of Scotland by the Romans, this formed part of the great " Caledonian Forest," and was cut down by the Roman army to drive the Caledonians from their retreats. This is abundantly proved by the Roman roads found on the clay, and in the neighbourhood of their camps. Many of the treè roots bear the marks of the axe as complete as they did nearly two thousand years ago, and considerable numbers the marks of fire; while some have been discovered around which were small stones, as if children had been at play. In consequence of the great masses of cut timber, and the natural softness of the soil, there could be no cultivation, if such a thing at that early period existed in Scotland; but, sheltered by the fallen trees, and nurtured by a salubrious climate, vegetation grew rank and strong; and as the seasons came and went, and years rolled on, the tall coarse grass sprung up, grew, and died, and as lair after lair fell and rotted, it added, however slowly, so much to the gradually increasing substance; and now, after the lapse of about two thousand years, we have that great mass of decayed vegetable matter called "moss."

To a sharp and experienced eye, each year's growth can be distinctly traced for several feet. At my request, a friend of mine made two different calculations of its apparent age, and the system followed was this:—He first took a part of the moss of an average depth, and carefully examined the lairs as far as possible; then, if a certain number of feet or inches gave so many years' growths, how many did the whole depth give? The first result was something more than eighteen hundred years, the second about twenty-one.

The "water of Guidi," now vulgarly called Goodie, which flows out of the Lake of Monteith, and washes the northern boundary of this moss, joins the Forth a little beyond its present termination, was anciently a lake, and in many old writs is styled the "Loch of Guidi," and on its bank stood the ancient Pictish city "Guidi." Here, in the eighth century, the Picts were attacked and routed by the Scots. The Scots in their turn were overpowered, and their country overrun by the Danes, who very naturally would introduce Danish names and customs, and there can be no doubt but the name "Flanders' Moss" is a corruption of some Danish word with which we are not familiar. The reverend editor of the " History of Stirlingshire," says it derives its name from the Danish " Flyn," a flat—" Flynder," a flat fish, &c.

Many interesting and valuable relics have been discovered under this moss. Graham of Duchray says, there was found in the year 1723, in the Forth, near Cardross, a large bone, between six and, seven feet long, one foot three inches thick, and one foot one inch broad. He also mentions the discovery of some immense horns—so large that a farmer used one of them as a foot-bridge over a *syvre* between his barn and byre. Two years ago, when cutting the moss to the east of the house of Cardross, what appeared to be the skeleton of a horse was brought to light, and at a depth of about fourteen feet below the surface. The bones were completely "mossised," being perfectly black, and were nearly all destroyed before being observed, part of the skull alone having been saved, which is now in the possession of a gentleman of antiquarian tastes. Beside the skeleton lay an entire hazel wand, which crumbled away on being exposed to the air. The fact of the stick would suggest the idea that man was present at the death. Not long ago part of an untanned cow-hide, with portions of hair adhering, was found on the clay beneath the moss on the estate of Cardross.

The most important and interesting discovery, however, made in this moss, was the laying bare, a few years ago, in the " Colniemoien" portion of it, of an ancient native encampment, made after the present gipsy fashion. The

K

different articles were found on the clay soil underneath
several feet of solid moss, the ribs of the tent or camp being still fixed in the clay. Their number could be counted,
and the round shape of the abode easily distinguished.
Adjoining the encampment were a considerable quantity of
bones completely blackened, and which crumbled away on
their exposure. Near it also was found an iron hammer,
with a round ring at the end for attaching to the girdle:
hammers of this kind were carried for close-quarter fighting.
In the immediate neighbourhood of the encampment were
discovered several pieces of peculiarly dressed wood, which,
when fitted together, made a complete and ingenious arm-
chair. Whether this was a Roman or native Caledonian
"tent" it is now impossible to tell. I should think, however, it is more likely to have been the abode for the time
being of a native family, and possibly attacked by invaders.
The fact of the bones would suggest this, they having all
the appearance of human bones—in all likelihood the remains of the inhabitants of the "tent." On the other hand,
the make of the hammer would lead us to believe that it
had belonged to a party considerably advanced in science,
above what the natives of that early period could be expected to be. A great number of Roman roads have been
laid bare from time to time under this moss; these, however, are generally observed in the vicinity of their "peels"
or encampments, and frequently passing between one
camp and another, and across the low marshes between
two higher grounds. The most perfect of these, in this
quarter, stretches from a camp which stood on the farm
of East Garden, under the moss, on Park's Farm, and
crosses the Forth below the house of Cardross.

THE ERSKINES OF CARDROSS.

IN trying to get at the foundation or origin of the illus-trious name of Erskine, we must go far back in the dark and misty track of history, and plod, inch by inch and foot by foot, the mazy pathway; we require to shake the dust off, and search the time-worn volumes that record the ex-ploits of heroic individuals, the deeds of great families, and the ups and downs of nations for well nigh a thousand years; and even then it is lost in dim antiquity. No house in Scotland—no family, either living or extinct—has given more sons to the camp, or produced men more eminent as statesmen, distinguished as lawyers, or will be more remem-bered in the flowery walks of literature, than the ancient and honourable house of Cardross. For hundreds of years this family have held, in a remarkable degree, the confidence of their various sovereigns; so much has this been the case, that few monarchs have reigned during the great historic period, without some of its members holding confident and exalted positions around the throne. In the country where their beautiful estate is situated, they have ever been ad-mired as possessing a true benevolence, a warmness of heart, and depth of friendship, combined with a liberality of sentiment, adorned by a meek humility, that spread a lustre over all their other accomplishments; and these latter gifts have descended, in a singular degree, to the present esteemed representative.

The origin of the name is traditionally assigned to the time of Malcolm the Second. At the battle of Murthill, a Scotch gentleman, by his daring and bravery, captured and decapitated Enrique the Danish general, and rushing towards the king with his dagger thrust through the hideous object, brandished it in the king's face, exclaiming in Gaelic, "Eris-Skyne," alluding to the deed, at the same time declaring he would perform greater deeds than that; whereupon the king at once conferred on him the surname of "Erskine." Most writers, however, think it probable that they at first derived their name from the barony of Erskine, on the Clyde, the property of the family for many ages; and it is through this line we intend to trace their history, through the Mar family, to the present representative.

I. Henricus de Erskine, proprietor of the above mentioned barony, and during the reign of Alexander the Second, was witness to a donation of Amelic—brother of Maldwin, Earl of Lennox—of the patronage of the church of Roseneath.

II. Sir John Erskine of Erskine, during the latter part of the reign of Alexander the Second, appears to have been proprietor of different lands in Renfrewshire. Johannes de Erskine is witness to a charter of Alexander III., in 1252, and another to the monastery of Paisley, by Walter, Earl of Menteith, of the church of Colmonell, in 1262. He left two sons, John and William. The latter obtained from his father a portion of land in Ayrshire, and confirmed by the superior, James, High Steward of Scotland.

III. John Erskine of Erskine, the eldest son, submitted to Edward I. of England. He left one son.

IV. Sir John, who does not appear to have been in any way distinguished. He had issue, one son (Sir William) and three daughters—1st, Mary, married first to Sir Thomas Bruce, brother of the renowned King Robert I.; he was taken prisoner by the English, and put to death; and she married, secondly, Sir Ingram Morville. 2d, Alice, married to Walter, High Steward of Scotland. 3d, Agnes, married to Sir William Livingston of Livingston.

V. Sir William, the only son, succeeded his father. He was a man of great bravery, and companion of the renowned Randolph, Earl of Moray, and the gallant Sir James Douglas. He accompanied the expedition into England in 1327, and for his valour was knighted under the royal banner. He died in the year 1329, leaving five sons. 1st, Sir Robert. 2d, Adam Erskine, of Barrowchan. 3d, Sir Allan, who had charters of the barony of Inchture in Perthshire, and Crambeth in Fife; and also held from King David II. the office crownarship of Fife and Fithyf. 4th, Andrew, who was granted, by King David II., with the crown lands of Raploch, near Stirling, in 1361.

VI. Sir Robert Erskine of Erskine, the eldest son, who appears to have been a man of most distinguished talents and accomplishments, and has rendered his name illustrious in his country's history. He early espoused the Brucean interest, by attaching himself to the High Steward and other friends of King David II., in opposition to the Baliol party, and was highly instrumental in its success. He was, by David II., appointed constable, keeper, and captain of Stirling Castle. He was appointed great chamberlain of the kingdom in 1350, and was one of the ambassadors to the court of England, to treat for the ransom of King David, after his capture in the battle of Durham. He also successfully brought about a truce between the two nations; and so great had he the interest of his prince and country at heart, that he gave his eldest son as an hostage for the payment of the ransom of his sovereign's deliverance. In 1358, he was appointed ambassador to the court of France, and ratified the alliance with that kingdom at Paris on the 29th June, 1359. He was five times sent on public business to England, between 1360 and 1364. He held the office of great justiciar north the Forth; and on the 17th of May, 1360, he presided at a solemn treaty upon the banks of that river, near Stirling, between the Drummonds of Drymen and the Menteiths of Ruskie. He was warder of the marches and heritable sheriff of Stirlingshire. He was also one of the Barones Mayores, who, in 1311, ratified Robert Stewart's succession to the crown; assisted at that monarch's coronation, and did homage to him at Scone. From this monarch and his predecessor he received extensive grants of land, viz.—Kinnoul, Malerbe, in Perthshire, Adamtoun in Ayrshire, and Kirkintilloch in Dumbartonshire. He was allowed twelve chalders of oatmeal out of the lands of Bothkennar, and two hundred merks sterling, annually, for the support of the castle, &c. Combined with his many accomplishments, he appears to have been possessed of a deep religious feeling, for we find him giving in "puer alms" to the monastery of Cambuskenneth, the patronage of the church of Kinnoul, with the lands of Fintalloch, in Strathearn, "for the health of himself and Christian Keith, his wife, while they lived, and the welfare of their souls after death." He died in the year 1385, and at his death Scotland lost one of her brightest ornaments. He married, first, Beatrice Lindsay, of the house of Crawford; and secondly, Christian, daughter of Sir John Menteith of Ruskie. He had issue by the former only. 1st, Sir Thomas, his successor; 2d, Sir Nicol, who was an ancestor to the Erskines of Kinnoul, in Perthshire, and which branch terminated in an heiress, who was married to Chrichton of Sanquhar, during the reign of James II.; 3d, Allan; and two daughters, the eldest of whom married Drummond of Concraig, and the youngest, Sir Walter Oliphant of Aberdalgy.

Sir Thomas Erskine, who was one of the hostages for the ransom of King David II., in the year 1357, succeeded his father in the year 1385. He was a gentleman of the greatest accomplishments and worth, and only a little less brilliant as a statesman, and useful to the nation, than his distinguished father. He succeeded his father as Governor of Stirling Castle; and, in 1384, he was appointed ambassador to England to treat for a promulgation of the truce between the two countries. That same year the English made a predatory excursion into the Frith of Forth, but were encountered by Sir Thomas and his brother Sir Nicol, and severely routed near North Queensferry.

In the year 1392 he was again, and during the reign of Robert III., sent ambassador to the court of England, and by that monarch he is styled "My dear relation." He held the charters of the barony of Dun, in Forfarshire, and Alloa, in Clackmannan.   He married Janet, daughter of Sir Edward Keith, Marischal of Scotland, and had issue two sons and two daughters.

1. Sir Robert, his successor.

2. Sir John, who obtained from his father the barony of Dun, and was ancestor of the Erskines of Dun, as also of Erskine of Brechin, who, during the reign of James V. became Secretary of State.

His daughters, Elizabeth and Christian, married Wemyss of Leuchars and Haldane of Gleneagles.

Sir Robert took a prominent part in the battle of Homildon, and had the misfortune to be taken prisoner.   Some time after his release, he was appointed one of the commissioners to treat for the release of James I. in 1421; and in 1424 he became one of the hostages for his ransom. His annual revenue at that time was valued at "1,000 merks."   He was released from captivity on the 19th June 1425; and on the death of the Earl of Mar, ten years later, he claimed that earldom, and assumed the title of Earl of Mar.   He married a daughter of the Lord of Lorn, and had issue one son and two daughters.

Thomas, his successor.

His daughter Janet married her relation Walter Stewart of Lovenax, second son of Murdoch, Duke of Albany, and who was executed at Stirling on the 24th May 1425, the day before the execution of his father and grandfather.

Elizabeth married Sir Henry Douglas of Loch-Leven.

Thomas, the first Earl of Mar of the name of Erskine, succeeded his father in the year 1453; but in 1457 he was by the assise of error dispossessed of the earldom, but held a charter of the lands of Dalnotter in Lennox. In the year 1458 he was employed in matters connected with the State, and was one of the guarantees of a treaty with the English. In 1467 he sat in Parliament, and took an active part in the cause of King James III. against his subjects, although previous to that time it appears that James had deprived him of his heritable right to keep the Castle of Stirling.

He was married to Lady Douglas, daughter of the Earl of Morton, and granddaughter of King James I. By her he had issue one son and three daughters, viz.—

Alexander, his successor.

Elizabeth, married to Sir Alexander Seton of Touch.

Mary, who married Sir William Livingston of Kilsyth.

Muriela, married to the Second Earl Marischal.

Alexander, second Lord Erskine, appears to have been a man of considerable influence. He had the charge of the youthful King James IV., and was a great favourite with that monarch ever afterwards. He was sworn a Privy Councillor, and appointed Governor of Dùmbarton Castle. He founded a chaplaincy in the church of Alloa for the welfare of the souls of King James III. and Christian Crichton, his deceased spouse, and for the health and prosperity of King James IV., himself, and Helen Home his then wife— (very charitable objects.) He received extensive grants of lands, and held the charters of the lands of Balhoghirty in Aberdeenshire, the lands of Nisbet and Douglas in Roxburghshire, the barony of Alway, the lands of Bernhills and Aulands, &c. &c.

He had married, first, a daughter of Sir Robert Crichton

of Sanquhar; and second, the eldest daughter of the first
Lord Home. He had issue by the former only, viz.—

1. Robert. 2. Alexander. 3. Walter, who was proprietor of Over Donnotars. 1. Christian, married to Sir David
Stewart of Rosyth. 2. Agnes, married to Sir William Menteith of Carse.

Robert, third Lord Erskine, does not appear to have been
a man of great talent or note, as we do not find him occu-
pying any very high position, or filling any situation of great
responsibility; farther than in 1506 he was made Sheriff
of Stirlingshire, and in 1513 fell with his sovereign at the
disastrous battle of Flodden. He married the eldest
daughter of Sir George Campbell of Loudoun, and had
issue five sons and four daughters, viz.—

1. Robert, who died young. 2. John. 3. James, who
held the charter of the lands of Little Sauchie. He was
ancestor of the Erskines of Balgony, and of William Erskine,
Bishop of Glasgow (who was knighted by King James IV.),
and grandfather of Janet, the countess of William, Earl of
Stirling. 4. Alexander, who appears to have been a clergyman. 5. William.

The daughters were—Catherine, married to Alexander,
second Lord Elphinston; Margaret, married first to Haldane of Gleneagles, second to George Home of Lundies
and Argaty; Elizabeth, married to Sir John Forrester of
Torwood; and Janet, married to John Murray of Touch-
adam.

John, fourth Lord Erskine, succeeded his father in 1513,
and like many of his illustrious ancestors, was one of the
great men of his time. In 1515 he was, by the Estates of

the kingdom, appointed ambassador to the court of France, for the purpose of endeavouring to get Scotland included in the French treaty with the English nation. Immediately after his return from the French capital, he was appointed governor of Stirling Castle, and intrusted with the high honour of the keeping of his young sovereign, King James V. In this delicate and difficult situation, he acquitted himself so much to the satisfaction of the monarch that he was high in the royal favour ever after. In 1517 he was one of the guarantees of a treaty with the English, and appointed constable and captain of the Castle of Stirling, and keeper of the King's Park, &c. In 1535 he was again appointed ambassador to France, for the purpose of arranging a marriage for his royal master. In 1539 he was constituted one of the extraordinary Lords of Session; and being present at the King's death, was, along with the Earl of Montrose, directed to remain continually with the young Queen in the Castle of Stirling. In 1545 Lords Erskine and Livingston were appointed keepers of the Queen's person; and after the disastrous battle of Pinkie (1547), they retired with their fair charge to the island of Inchmahome, on the Lake of Monteith, where they remained till the end of February of the following year, when they set sail from Dumbarton for France. In France he is said to have discharged his high and difficult duty with the greatest fidelity and prudence. Dying in 1552, he left extensive estates. He married Lady Margaret Campbell, daughter of the Earl of Argyll, by whom he had issue:—

1. Robert, Master of Erskine, who married Lady Margaret Graham, eldest daughter of the second Earl of Mon-

trose. He was taken prisoner at Solway in 1543, but was ransomed for two hundred pounds, and was afterwards killed at the battle of Pinkie. He had no legitimate issue, but a natural son by Mrs. Jean Home, who was commentator of Dryburgh, and ancestor of the Erskines of Sheffield.

2. Thomas, Master of Erskine, who was ambassador to England. He was married to Margaret, daughter of Lord Fleming, the Chamberlain of Scotland, but by her he had no family. He had a natural son, who was commentator of Cambuskenneth, but died before his father, in 1551.

3. John, who succeeded his father.

4. Sir Alexander Erskine of Gogar, ancestor of the Earls of Kellie.

5. Sir James Erskine of Tullibody.

1. Elizabeth, who married Sir Walter Seton of Touch.

2. Margaret, who had a natural child to James V. viz. James, Earl of Moray, Regent of Scotland.

John, fifth Lord Erskine, was a man of transcendant genius. He held many high offices, and was remarkable for disinterestedness, love of country, and attachment to Protestantism. Being a younger brother, he was trained to the Church; and, previous to his father's death, he had been appointed by King James V. commentator of Cambuskenneth and Inchmahome. On coming into possession of the title and estates, he also succeeded to his heritable offices, and to the government of Edinburgh Castle. During the troublous times of the Queen Regent, he maintained a strict neutrality, by standing aloof from either party. On the advance of the English in 1560, the Queen committed herself to his lordship's protection; and

on the return, in the following year, of the young Queen
Mary from France, his lordship was sworn a Privy Councillor, and restored to the ancient title of Earl of Mar,
and accordingly took his seat in Parliament as representing
the most ancient earldom in the kingdom.   On the birth
of King James VI., the Queen mother committed her
infant son to the keeping of the Earl of Mar, who resigned
the Castle of Edinburgh to the Bothwell party, and retired
to Stirling Castle.   In 1571, when the Regent Lennox was
surprised and killed at Stirling, it was only through the
prompt and decisive character of Mar that the King's
party were saved from utter annihilation.   Immediately
after this great achievement he was chosen Regent of
the kingdom, and this important trust was conferred on
him for "his moderation, his humanity, and his disinterestedness."   On finding himself in possession of this high
and difficult office, he set himself with all the ardour of his
mind to allay the different contending factions, and to free
his beloved country from the influences of foreign councils.
For a time he seemed eminently successful, but the vile
Morton thwarted his views.   The ambition and selfishness
of Morton and his associates made a deep impression
on the Regent's mind, who longed for peace and the
full prosperity of his country; and this grief bringing on
a settled melancholy, he died of a broken heart on the
29th October 1572.   Thus passed away for the time one
of Scotland's most gifted sons—whose mind was too pure
and heart too large for the age in which he lived.   He was
married to Annabella, daughter of Sir William Murray of
Tullibardine, and had issue:—

John, his successor; and

Lady Mary, who married Archibald, eighth Earl of Angus.

John, seventh Earl of Mar, was a man of great talent and education, having been trained along with King James VI. by the celebrated George Buchanan, and was high in royal favour ever after. In 1595, he was intrusted with the keeping and education of the King's son; in 1601, he was appointed English ambassador; and, on the death of Queen Elizabeth, he completed the arrangements for the succession of the Scotch monarch to the English throne, in 1603. In that year he accompanied his sovereign to England, but was obliged to return to arrange with the Queen regarding the keeping of her children. After appeasing the Queen, he again set out for England, to join his royal master; and immediately on his arrival in London he was sworn a Privy Councillor, created a Knight of the Garter, and became Secretary for Foreign Affairs; and on the 17th December 1615, the King delivered to him the "white staff," appointing him High-Treasurer of Scotland. Previous to this, about the year 1604, King James, anxious to confer some permanent mark of honour on his distinguished subject, created him Lord Cardross, with power to assign the title to any of his heirs male; and from the Parliamentary records it appears in the Parliament held at Perth, 19th July 1606, "Act of erection of the Abbey of Dryburgh and Cambuskenneth and Priory of Inchmahome into a temporal lordship, called 'the lordship of Cardross,' in favour of the Earl of Mar—with the honour, estate, dignity, and pre-eminence of a free Lord of Parliament; to be called Lord Cardross in all time coming." Some time before the

year 1617, he built the principal suit of apartments in
Cardross House; and when the King came to Scotland in
that year he visited Lord Cardross, at Cardross House,
where he was entertained for some days with the greatest
respect and magnificence. This great statesman died at
Stirling in the year 1634, in the 77th year of his age. His
lordship married, first, a daughter of the second Lord
Drummond, by whom he had issue one son, John, who
succeeded to the earldom of Mar. He married, secondly,
Lady Mary Stuart, second daughter of the Duke of Lennox,
her ladyship having a charter of the lands of Fintry and
Buchlyvie. By her he had issue four sons—1st, James,
who married Lady Mary Douglas, Countess of Buchan, and
was created Earl of Buchan; 2d, Henry Erskine, to whom
his father assigned the peerage of Cardross; 3d, Sir Alexander Erskine, a colonel in the army, and who had the misfortune to be blown up at Dunglass, along with his unfortunate brother-in-law, the Earl of Haddington, in 1640;
and 4th, Sir Alexander Erskine of Alva.

In a life of this illustrious man, written by the Earl of
Buchan, there is rather a curious anecdote told relating to
his second marriage. It appears that the Earl, although
one of the most advanced men of his time, had been somewhat superstitious, and had listened to the nonsense of an
Italian conjuror, who had shown him the limning of a lady,
whom he said resembled Mar's future sweetheart and countess. Mar, it seems, had been in love with the daughter of
Lennox, and fancied he saw her likeness in the portrait ex-
hibited by the Italian. Fearing disappointment, and hearing
that the King intended her for another, his Lordship wrote

a touching letter to his royal master, couched in the most plaintive language, stating that his health had begun to fail through the fear of losing the object of his affections. The King, it is said, visited his old class-fellow, and said—"Ye shana dee, Jock, for ony lass in a' the land," and accordingly secured for him Lady Mary Stuart. Portraits of this distinguished man and his celebrated lady are still preserved in Cardross House, along with that of the Treasurer's father.

Henry Erskine, the second son of the Earl of Mar, by his second marriage, to whom the peerage of Cardross was assigned, with the reservation of his father's life-rent, having died before his father, never possessed the title. He held charters of the ecclesiastical lands of Maxtown and Lessudden, in Roxburghshire, and in which he is designed " fiar of Cardross." He was married to the only daughter of Sir James Bellenden Broughton, and had issue:—

David, second Lord Cardross; and Mary, married to Sir John Buchanan of Buchanan.

In one respect, the peerage of Cardross stands unexampled in the history of the Peerage, inasmuch as the King conferred upon a subject the right to create another peer, which has never been done in any other instance.

David, second Lord Cardross, succeeded his grandfather in the year 1634, and became vested in the title of Cardross. He appears to have been a man of considerable note, and took a prominent part in many of the nation's affairs. At Newcastle, in 1646, he protested, with a few more peers, against the delivering up of King Charles I. to the English army; he was one of the promoters of the engagement in 1648, for which he was fined in one thousand pounds, besides losing his seat in Parliament. He died in the year 1671. He married, first, Anne, fifth daughter of Sir Thomas Hope of Craighall; and had two children—Henry, third Lord Cardross; and Margaret, married to Cunningham of Boquhan. His lordship married, secondly, Mary, youngest daughter of Sir George Bruce of Carnock, and sister of the Earl of Kincardine, and had issue seven children:—1. Hon. Alexander Erskine, who appears to have died young. 2. Hon. Colonel William Erskine, who was a man of the greatest integrity and honour. He was proprietor of the estate of Torry, and governor of Blackness Castle. He married a daughter of Sir James Lumsdain of Innergelly. His son William was a person of considerable note, having been a colonel in the army, and distinguished himself at the battle of Fontenoy, where he commanded the 7th regiment of dragoons.

3. The Hon. Colonel John Erskine of Cardross, known among his friends as "the Black Colonel." The Colonel was distinguished for his zeal in the high cause of religion and liberty, and for which he suffered keen persecution, and was compelled to retire into Holland. In Holland he had the command of a company of foot; and at the Revolution of 1688 he accompanied the Prince of Orange to England. He was ever afterwards a great favourite with the Prince, who made him Governor of Stirling and Dumbarton Castles. He represented the town of Stirling in the last Scottish Parliament, was a keen supporter of the Union, and one of the Members nominated to the first united Parliament of Great Britain in 1707. At the general election in 1708, he was again re-chosen to repre-

sent the town of Stirling. He died at Edinburgh in 1742, in the eighty-second year of his age. He was four times married, and was father of John Erskine of Carnock, Advocate, author of that valuable work, "Erskine's Institutes of the Law of Scotland."

4. The Hon. Charles Erskine, who was killed at the battle of Steinkirk in 1692.

–The daughters were Veronica, married to Lockhart of Kirktown; Magdalen, married to Alexander Monypenny of Pitmilly; and Mary, who died young.

Henry, third Lord Cardross, succeeded his father in 1671. He was a man of the most pure principles and exalted worth, having received a highly religious education. Trained in the broad principles of truth and liberty, he early joined himself to the opposers of the Earl of Lauderdale's Administration; but, for his adherence to the cause he had so much at heart, he was subjected to the most keen and cruel persecution, and in 1674, for his lady hearing her own chaplain preach in her own house, he was fined in the modest sum of "five thousand pounds." In May of the following year, while absent in Edinburgh, a party of soldiers came to Cardross during midnight, plundered the house, and subjected Lady Cardross to the most barbarous usage. In August of the same year he was, for his adherence to the cause of truth, sentenced to be imprisoned in Edinburgh for the period of four years. In 1677 he was again fined on account of his lady getting her child baptised by a person not her own parish minister, notwithstanding his Lordship being then in prison and not allowed to look after his affairs. In 1677 his estates in East Lothian were plundered by the King's troops. In July of the same year his Lordship was released from prison on granting a bond for the amount of his fine. Not being able to obtain any redress from the Privy Council of Scotland, his Lordship repaired to North America, where he was only a little more fortunate—a colony which he founded having been destroyed by the Spaniards. He left America, and, joining the Prince of Orange party in Holland, he accompanied the Prince to England, where he was appointed to the command of a troop of dragoons. He was afterwards a great favourite with King William, was sworn a Privy Councillor, and constituted General of the Mint, &c. He died at Edinburgh in May 1693, in the 42d year of his age. He married a daughter of Sir William Stewart of Kirkhill, and had issue:—

1. David, fourth Lord Cardross.

2. Hon. Charles Erskine, Advocate. He married the heiress of Scott of Redenshead, in Fife.

3. Hon. William Erskine, Governor of Blackness Castle. He married Margaret, daughter of Colonel Erskine, Governor of Stirling Castle.

4. Hon. Thomas Erskine, Advocate. He married Rachel, daughter and heir of Liberton of Liberton.

The daughters were—1. The Hon. Catherine Erskine, who married Sir William Denholm of Westershields, in the county of Lanark. 2. Hon. Mary Erskine, who married James Nimmo, Esq., Cashier of Excise. 3. Hon. Anne Erskine, who married Edmonstone of Duntreath.

David, fourth Lord Cardross, succeeded his father in 1693. Like most of his predecessors, he took an active part in State affairs, was a true Protestant, and took a deep interest in the Hanoverian succession. About the year 1698 his Lordship succeeded to the Earldom of Buchan, and was afterwards known under that title. He was a Privy Councillor, and one of the Council of Trade appointed by Parliament in the year 1705. In the all-important question of the Union, his Lordship opposed the material clauses, and lodged his protest accordingly. This action, however, caused his removal from all his Government offices. When King George I. came to the throne, the Earl of Buchan was made Lord-Lieutenant of the Counties of Stirling and Clackmannan. During the Rebellion of 1715 he held the town of Stirling and commanded the Stirlingshire Militia. In the year 1745 his Lordship sold the estate of Cardross to his cousin, John Erskine of Carnock, the Advocate, and author of " Erskine's Institutes," who was the first Mr. Erskine of Cardross and Carnock. This "distinguished civilian" died at Cardross on the 1st March, 1768, in the 73d year of his age. He married, first, Miss Melville, daughter of the Earl of Leven and Melville, and had issue—John Erskine of Carnock, D.D., a zealous and distinguished pastor. He married, secondly, Anne, daughter of Stirling of Keir, and had issue four sons and two daughters:—

  1. James Erskine, who was the first " Mr. Erskine of Cardross."

  2. Robert Erskine, who died in the East Indies.

  3. David Erskine, who was a Writer to the Signet, and of great eminence in his profession.

  4. Major Erskine of Venlaw, in Peebles.

The daughters were:—1. Marion, died unmarried; 2. Christian, who married Sir William Stirling of Ardoch.

James Erskine succeeded his father in the estate of Cardross, and died there on the 27th March 1802. He married Lady Christian Bruce, second daughter of the Earl of Kincardine, and had issue:—

1. John Erskine, an officer in the E. I. C. service, and who died at Angole in 1792.

2. William Erskine, who died young.

3. Charles, who commanded the gallant 92d Regiment in the expedition to Egypt, under the renowned Sir Ralph Abercromby, and was mortally wounded at the landing of the British troops near Alexandria.

4. David Erskine of Cardross.

5. James, an officer in the Royal Navy, and who unfortunately perished on board Lord Keith's flag-ship, burned in March 1800.

6. William Erskine, a Major in the 71st Foot, who died in 1805.

The daughters were:—1. Janet, married to Hay of Drummelgier. 2. Anne. 3. Marion. 4. Matilda, married to John Graham of Gartur, the last and only cadet of note of the defunct Earldom of Monteith. 5. Rachael Euphemia. 6. Christian.

David Erskine of Cardross was bred to the profession of the law, and was some time in the civil service of the E. I. C. at Ceylon. He died about the year 1848. He married the Hon. Keith Elphinstone, fourth daughter of John, 11th Lord Elphinstone, and had issue:—

1. James, who was in the civil service at Bombay, but

who died before his father, leaving two sons:—1. The present Major Erskine of Cardross. 2. Captain James Erskine, of the Royal Navy.

2. John Elphinstone Erskine, Admiral, Royal Navy, and the talented author of "The Islands of the Western Pacific," and at present the accomplished M.P. for the county of Stirling.

3. Charles, a Captain in the Army, but who was unfortunately killed by a fall from his horse while serving with his regiment in India.

4. George Keith, Captain of the 1st Lancers, a gentleman of great accomplishments, and elegant manners, but who unfortunately died of small-pox, while serving with his regiment at the siege of Mooltan in 1849. His brother officers raised a beautiful tablet to his memory in the tomb at Cardross.

5. Hay M. Erskine, an esteemed Clergyman.

6. William Erskine, a Captain in the Bombay Army, who died, leaving two daughters.

Henry David Erskine, the present esteemed proprietor, is married to Horatio, daughter of General Seymour, and has two children.

"GARDEN."

AMONG the many fertile, beautiful, and richly cultivated estates of the county of Stirling, none is more pleasantly associated, nor holds a higher place, than the ancient and interesting estate of Garden.

The mansion-house is beautifully situated on a commanding eminence at the foot of the sequestered glen of Arngibbon, one of the prettiest retreats in the west of Scotland. The spacious park in which the house stands is carefully adorned with grand old trees, rearing high their princely heads, and spreading wide their giant boughs, that have for ages welcomed the zephyrs of summer, and borne unscathed the hurricanes of winter, while conspicuous among their fellows stand some of the very finest silver firs in the kingdom.

The old castle of Garden stood a little to the north of where the present mansion is built, and on a small eminence in what was in early times a small lake, but now a fertile meadow. The castle was of the circular tower form, and in feudal days must have been considered impregnable, having been surrounded by water, and protected by a draw-bridge. · Some distance to the north-west of the old castle was the "gallows-hill," where poor offending wretches "gat the rape;" and, in the memory of some of the oldest inhabitants, there was to be seen a stone with an inscription denoting the felons' names who ignominiously perished.

The glen of Arngibbon is about two miles in length, and may be termed "beautiful and interesting" rather than grand. The lower portion is finely ornamented with large trees of various kinds; and, farther on, the slopes are covered with fine young copsewood. Here the geologist may explore, the botanist roam, and the naturalist find instruction; while the lover of Nature's beauties can admire the feathered banks that rise around him, and gaze on the fern-covered rocks that overhang his head in shattered masses, the moss and lichen clinging for life and sustenance to their brown faces—or look at the crystal stream as it tumbles over its rocky bed at his feet;—

> " For o'er thy crags, with sullen roar,
>   The moorland waters loudly pour,
>   Leaping on from rock to rock,
>   Till plunging o'er with sullen shock,
>   It weareth deep the cavern riven,
>   That opes her yawning jaws to heaven."

In several parts of the glen there are beautiful little cascades, the largest one being at the top, where the water from the moorland heights tumbles over a rock about fourteen feet high, forming a delightful pool beneath. Around, the rocks rise to a height of about sixty feet, their faces covered with lichen and fern, and their tops crowned with fantastic roots. At their base the wrecks of ages, torn from their slopes by the suns of summer and the winds of winter, lie scattered in the bed of the turbulent stream, washed by the waters of a thousand years.

By the kind permission of the proprietor, this exquisite

retreat is left open to all who use the privilege with pro-
priety; and I know of no other place where one can spend
a leisure hour or two with more pleasure and profit than in
the glen of Arngibbon. Here, in the quiet eventide, you
can hearken to the hoarse croak of the raven, as it perches
on some giant bough, or view it as it soars in beautiful
circles high overhead, or listen to the feathered warblers
as they chant their evening hymn, and fill the air with their
melodies. You can watch the finny-tribe as they sportive
play in the pool, walled with granite and paved with rock.
You can trace the wanderings of the tawny owl, as it feeds
its tender young on yon shelving crag, and again goes a
roving after other-prey.

A little above the village of Arnprior stood the old castle
of Arnfinlay, now completely erased.

The village of Arnprior is now solely the property of
Mr. Stirling of Garden, and the stranger visiting it will not
be disappointed. There is a commanding view of the vale
of Monteith; and should he wish to see some of "my
friends" in their glory, he ought to meet them after their
third tumbler, when

> "It kindles wit, it waukens lair,
> It bangs us fou o' knowledge."

Adjoining the village is the beautiful little glen of that
name, rendered for ever classic by the residence on its banks
of Buchanan of Arnprior, the famous "King o' Kippen," and
his descendants. This glen very much resembles that of Arngibbon, and need not be described. It is, however, remark-
ably interesting, and well repays a visit, the only drawback
being that the walks have been allowed to disappear.

MONTEITH.

ALAS, Monteith! where's now thy name,
Thy ancient glory, and thy fame?
In thee, when reign'd thy halcyon morn,
Old Scotia's truest sons were born.
Stewart, and Drummond, and the Græme—
Who swelled the foremost ranks of fame—
Saw first the light within thy strand,
And first brought honour to thy land,
When Norway, teeming with her hosts,
Launched bearded hordes on Largu's coasts,
The Stewart, from their native heath,
Led forth thy bravest sons, Monteith;
And there, amid the battle tide,
Smote the grim Norseman in the Clyde.
When Bruce, who hated Edward's sway,
Whispered brave Drummond to the fray,
From mountain, lake, and river side
Burst forth that glorious living tide
That, fighting for an empire just,
Laid England's legions in the dust;
And gave them still a mightier urn
In the dread trench at Bannockburn
The Græme—his name is wide and far
In deeds of honour and of war,
And needs not my poor humble spell
To waft his fame, his glories tell;—
Suffice it that his spirit still
Hallows the lonely lake and hill.
But fortune fair has ceased to smile:
Gray ruin reigns on every isle!—
Talla is now a mouldering dome,
Glory has fled from Inchmahome;

There's now no smile of monarch there,
Nor din of courtiers fill the air;
No chieftains meeting, as of yore,
Nor sturdy clansmen tread the shore;
No march of warriors round Porten',
Nor sound of pibroch in the glen.
The fiery cross has ceased to fly;
No signal on Crochmelly high
Doth fling its glare athwart the night,
To gather clansmen to the fight;
Or tell the men of Aberfoyle
That neighbouring clans invade the soil.
No sign of strife along the hill;
Mondhuie's slopes are quiet and still;
No war-cry, heard across yon brake,
Returns its echoes from the Lake;
No sound of hunters, with the horn,
Breaks the soft stillness of the morn;
Nor wide the hounds their echoes fling,
To start the game from out Milling,
Where, deep amid the Claggan dell,
The last fierce wolf of Scotland fell;
And where, amid thy tangled fold,
Brave monarchs chased the deer of old,
The fox was killed on yonder steep,
The otter in the reedy deep,
The stag within the brake was sought,
And from Craigvad the wolf was brought.
In Calziemuck's deep shades alane,
The wild boar stood and shook his mane;
And, far among the copse profound
He bade defiance to the hound,
Till, issuing from the thicket clear,
He yielded to the Royal spear.
    But, though those scenes have passed away,
And higher honours seen decay,
A shadowy grandeur gleams beneath
The faded glories of Monteith.
The Lake, the glen, the rock, the hill—
Monteith, Monteith remaineth still!
Come with me, then: in fancy's flight
Be guided to yon heathery height,

Where nature in her beauty lies,
And tell me if its glory dies!
When the red sun has upwards worn,
And burst as on creation's morn—
When his first ray doth tint the rills
That gurgle down the Lennox hills;
And finny tribes, deep in the pool,
Are sporting 'mid the waters cool—
Where moor-cock's cry among the heath
Is the lone watchword in Monteith.
No smoke ascends from Rednock walls;
No voices gladden Cardross halls;
Gartmore is silent 'neath the hill,
And Auchentroig doth slumber still;
No peasant stalks along Garden—
Perchance, some smuggler in the glen,
With thoughts of awe and secret pleasure,
Is watching o'er unlawful treasure.

The morn has chased the night away;
Now wakens many a bird of prey.
The cormorant has left the reeds,
And greedy on the lake she feeds;
While round her, in their downy coat,
Her tender offspring gently float.
The wild swan through the free air swings
And takes the zephyrs in her wings;
Her neck thrown back, with prideful ease
She silent sails before the breeze.
From jutting crag, the falcon keen
Scans with bright eye the hunting scene;
His wings he fans; then taking flight,
Spies heron in a lonely bight;
But, as he hangs 'tween earth and sky,
The victim shrinks with fear and cry;
A moment crouching in despair,
The long-wing'd creature takes the air.
Then down the noble falcon sweeps,
Up still the stately heron keeps;
Swoop after swoop he tries the game,
But ah! brave bird, you miss your aim.
Up, and far up, they rise to view—
The battle deepens 'mid the blue;

Till to the clouds the prey birds rise—
Another swoop—the heron dies!
When noble osprey leaves her nest
And tender young on yon high crest,
And heavenward swiftly soars away
Into the brightening dawn of day,
She floats beyond the reedy brake,
And hovers, fate-like, o'er the lake:
Then meteor-like she falls, and lo
Her scaly victim feels the blow:
. Now soaring up, with victor's cry,
Triumphant bears the prey on high;
And far beyond the hunter's ken,
She feeds her eaglets in their den.

   Wake, traveller, from your couch and sweep
Fearless around yon rugged steep,
Where, with sheer front and crown of stone,
Bendarack rears her head alone.
Then mark, before your awe-struck eyes,
The glories that around you rise!
Turn northward, and before you view
The glorious land of Roderick Dhu—
A land that, 'mid the fastness green,
Of old hid many an outlaw keen.
Land of Vich Alpine's daring clan!
The scourge of foemen, and the ban
Of cruel tyrants that around
Track'd the Macgregor with the hound;
Till, springing from the trodden race,
A chieftain rose of conquering pace:
Whose name sharp time can ne'er destroy—
The name and memory of Rob Roy!
Gaze westward, and, adorned with rills,
Lo, Aberfoyle's gray shattered hills,
Ben-Lomond, far above the rest,
Rears proudly his imperial crest:
Hid oft in clouds from mortal view,
Oft shining in the summer blue.
See, robed within his morning cloud,
Like giant in his ghastly shroud,
Ben-Dhu his awful vigils keep,
Where Chon's dark waters slumber deep,

There, quiet amid her reedy home,
The prowling otters safely roam;
And, guarded 'mid the rocky hill,
The native wild-cat lingers still.
Beneath the crags in yonder glen,
She tends her young within her glen;
Then leads them out from day to day,
To scour the heather for their prey.
Proudly among wild nature's store
Stands up thy rugged form, Craigmore,
Which, sentry-like, doth watch and ward
The secret glories of Loch-Ard;
And, like some veteran from the field,
Who long hath wielded spear and shield,
And only dreameth now of wars,
While nature heals his glorious scars;
And, resting on his laurels true,
He overshadows dark Avondhu.
Onward and southward lies the plain:
With parks, and trees, and waving grain—
As sweet a realm as eye may see
In golden land of Arcady.
The lake beneath, untouched by gale,
Reposes like a fairy dale;
While, stretching onwards in their pride,
The Forth and Endrick roll their tide.
Dark Forth, from yonder tiny rill
Doth gather strength from every hill,
Till, flowing through bright links of glee,
It swells into a frith and sea.
Proud Endrick, from yon mountain crest,
Rolleth her stream into the west,
Still strengthened by the foaming rills
That gurgle from a hundred hills;
It whirls along from rock to rock,
Then, plunging o'er with sullen shock,
It weareth deep yon cavern lone,
Where winds and falling waters moan;
And, gathering strength from every fen,
This silver river sweeps the glen,
And, flowing on through field and brake,
It leaps into sweet Lomond's lake.

Far onward, in the distant blue,
Dumgoyne doth rear his shoulders true,
And, like some watchman on the strand,
Proudly surveys the nether land—
Above each hill and hidden den
Watching the wilds of Sochy-glen,
(The robber's secret haunt of yore,
Still famous in romantic lore)
His giant form doth stand alane
The misty guardian of Strathblane.
Old Gartmore from amidst her bowers
Uplifts to heaven her aged towers.
Gartartan, 'mid thy dungeons deep
The spirits nightly revels keep;
And ghosts of those that went the way
When Gartmore barons held the sway,
Wander among thy vaults at will,
And haunt thy dismal chambers still.
There's yet the "pin" amid the gloom
That sent the felons to their doom;
And, hanging on the mouldering walls,
The hellish tackling still appals.*
Lo, eastward, wreathed like the main,
The mist is rolled along the plain;
While in the strath each knoll and tree
Seem islands in a lonely sea;
And yonder, like some distant sail
Craigforth breaks through the misty veil,
While Stirling, with her head on high,
Holds converse with the summer sky;
And far beyond, amid the blue,
Proud Sal'sbury Crags crown up the view.
  Come, wander with me on the shore
Where evening shades the landscape o'er,
The vernal day has gone to rest;
The heavenly orb sinks in the west;
The mist is lingering o'er the fen,
The night-hawk cries within the glen;

* In the memory of some of the old parties of the district, the " gibbet-pin" and some other of the items required for "neck-twisting" adorned the old walls of Gartartan Castle.

The shepherd boy the flaming brand
Displays within his tiny hand,
And in a moment, at his will,
With fire and smoke enwraps the hill:
From neuk and corry brightly glare
The fiery tongues that lap the air—
On, on and up it spreads with ease
Its broad red wing upon the breeze.
The peasant lad doth wander then
To meet his mistress in the glen;
And as he slowly stalks along,
The shepherd's daughter chants her song;
Which on the balmy zephyr floats,
In every grove are heard the notes:
They echo sweet along the fell
And whisper backward from the dell,
And as they touch his ear again,
Enraptured stands the love-sick swain.
When evening doth succeed the day,
The moon has chased the sun away,
And from the east doth upward rise,
And in her sweet course floods the skies;
While little starlets in her wake
Reflect their glories in the lake;
Then, all alone, oh! take the oar,
And push your boatie from the shore,
And steering through the waters, guide
Your shallop o'er the rippling tide,
Till, at yon fairy point you land,
Then pace along the islet strand,
And in a sweet poetic swoon
View the calm ruins by the moon.
In gloomy form, 'tween earth and skies,
The dark monastic ruins rise.
Go wander round the crumbling walls,
And peer into the roofless halls.
With fairy step then gently creep
To where the ancient heroes sleep,
And as the gate doth backward roll
A silent awe will fill thy soul,
And tell thee thou should'st lightly tread
In presence of the sacred dead.

Around those early heroes rest
These sculptured stones upon their breast,
To tell the wanderer of their fame,
Their ancient lineage and their name.
Beneath yon slab, with warrior crest,
The noble Drummond's ashes rest,
Buckled in his good sword and shield,
The hero trimmed for battle-field—
Trampling the lions valiantly,
His coat of arms the surging sea.
Perchance the moon her shadow throws
Where Stuart and his spouse repose—
Calm, arm in arm the man and wife.
Lie sculptured to the very life—
Her arm beneath his head doth rest,
His hand is gloved upon her breast—
Sleeping upon one pillow there,
How sweetly rest the wedded pair!
Around thee lie great men of fame,
The sons of many a " gallant Graham,"
Who led the van, and won with might
The palm of many a gory fight:
Though dead beneath these tablets hoary,
They live, they live in Scotland's story!

M

THE STIRLINGS OF GARDEN.

IN every country and in every district there are certain families of distinction—those grand old landmarks of society that more or less adorn every country. In times of war and trouble, the clansmen and followers would gather around them for advice, to resent an insult or to repel an invader; and in times of "peace and plenty," headed by their chief, they would assemble round the festive board and social cup, and there cement the bond of union and friendship between the ruled and those that rule. Now, there is no nation in the world more proverbial for these adornments than dear old Scotland, and no district has produced more families of distinction than Stirlingshire; while there is no family in the county more remarkable for their endearing social natures, sterling worth, and love of country, than the ancient family of Garden.

It may be said this branch of the Stirlings has not produced any members distinguished in history, or that will be known to posterity; but for hundreds of years the family has been remarkable, as possessing a stern integrity and honesty of purpose, and an attachment to the institutions of the country rarely to be met with; and has at least produced two members of singular ability and distinction;

while we look upon the young chief of the house as possessed of some of the rarest gifts of his honoured ancestry.

This branch of the Stirling family have held Garden since about the beginning of the seventeenth century. The first proprietor of Garden, of the name of Stirling, was Sir Archibald Stirling of Keir, who purchased the estate from Sir James Forrester of Garden, of the very ancient family of that name. At that time the estate is said to have comprehended East, Middle, and West Garden, and is so noted in " Pont's map of the Lennox."

1: The first of the family who possessed Garden as a separate estate was Sir John Stirling, Knight, second son of Sir Archibald Stirling of Keir, who received it from his father in 1613, on the occasion of his marriage.*

.2. Sir Archibald Stirling succeeded his father, Sir John. He was educated at the University of Glasgow, and became a very distinguished student. He afterwards became a member of the various Committees of War, appointed for the defence of the country in 1643. He also obtained the command of a troop of horse under the Earl of Lanark in the year 1648. He was fined £1,500 sterling by Cromwell's Act of Grace, and pardoned 1654. On the 14th of February 1661, he was nominated one of the Senators of the College of Justice, when he assumed the title of " Lord Garden." He was chosen a Lord of the Articles in 1661 and 1663.

. He married, first, a daughter of Sir Patrick Murray of Elibank. The issue by this marriage was two sons and two daughters:—

* The Stirlings of Keir and their Family Papers.

1. John, who succeeded to the Keir estate.

2. George, who died young, but another son received the same name in 1653.

3. Anna, born at Garden on 3d August 1634.

4. Margaret, born at Stirling 9th January 1660.

He married, secondly, a daughter of Sir James Murray of Kilbaberton, and had issue—seven sons and three daughters:—

1. Archibald, born at Garden 21st March 1651, who succeeded his father in the Garden estate.

2. James, who married a daughter of Sir George Stirling of Glorat.

3. George, born at Ochiltree 20th July 1653.

4. William, born at Ochiltree 20th October 1654.

5. Alexander, born at Ochiltree 26th December 1656.

6. Thomas, born at Ochiltree 25th December 1658.

7. Henry, born at Edinburgh 20th July 1667, was an Ensign in the Company raised by the London Merchants for duty in the East Indies.

8. Catherine, born at Edinburgh 8th September 1647.

9. Elizabeth, born at Ochiltree 31st January 1649.

10. Rebecca, born at Ochiltree 2d April 1650.

3. Archibald Stirling succeeded his father, Lord Garden, in the year 1668. This Laird of Garden was a very prominent man of his time. He was a keen supporter of the Stuart family; and, along with his retainers from Garden, swelled the assembly known in history and tradition as the "Gathering of the Brig of Turk." For his zeal in the cause of his sovereign, he was apprehended, carried to London for examination before the Privy Council, and

imprisoned in Newgate till the month of July. He was then sent back to Edinburgh Castle, and tried for high treason, but acquitted. He married, first, Margaret Bailie, only daughter of Sir Gideon Bailie of Lochend, and widow of Sir John Colquhoun of Luss, by whom he had issue—an only son, Archibald, who succeeded to the estate of Garden. This amiable lady died at Garden, 20th July, 1679. By her former marriage with Sir John Colquhoun, she was mother of Lilias Colquhoun, wife of Sir John Stirling of Keir, elder brother of Archibald Stirling of Garden. The wives of the two brothers were accordingly mother and daughter, the younger brother being married to the mother.

Archibald Stirling married, secondly, the eldest daughter of Sir Alexander Hamilton of Haggs, who had issue four sons and five daughters.

1. James, who died in early life.

2. John, who acquired the estate of Garden from his eldest brother Archibald, in 1718.

3. James, one of the most distinguished Mathematicians of his time; the bosom friend of Sir Isaac Newton; and the companion and correspondent of all the great philosophers of his day.

4. Charles, who was a merchant in Jamaica.

The daughters appear to have all died young or unmarried.

Archibald Stirling died at Garden in 1715, aged sixty-four, having possessed the estate forty-eight years.

4. Archibald, the only son of the first marriage, succeeded his father in the estate of Garden. He was a man of considerable learning, and went to Barbadoes as private

tutor in the family of Judge Walker. He sold the estate of Garden to his next brother, about a year after his succession.

5. John Stirling of Garden, who acquired the estate of Garden from his brother, built the present mansion-house on the lands then called Blairfeichan. He married Grizel Graham, youngest daughter of Robert Graham of Gartmore, and had issue three sons and two daughters:—

1. Archibald, who succeeded to the estate.

2. Robert, who was in the Indian army, but died at the Cape of Good Hope, while on his homeward journey in 1765.

3. James, who was a West India planter, but died in Jamaica, young and unmarried.

4 and 5. Isobel and Ann both died unmarried.

6. Archibald Stirling of Garden succeeded his father in 1760. He was a man of the most energetic mind; for a time he assisted his uncle in the management of the extensive mines at Leadhills, and on the death of his relative succeeded to the sole management. He much improved the estate of Garden, and purchased the adjoining properties of Arngibbon and Arnfinlay. He married his cousin, the daughter of James Stirling the Mathematician, and had issue one son. He died at Garden 1829, aged eighty-seven years.

7. James Stirling of Garden. He greatly improved the estate, having during his lifetime expended no less a sum than £40,000 in extending and improving the property; and purchased the adjoining estate of Arnmore. He was a gentleman of the most honourable and upright character,

and one of the most kind and warm-hearted landlords in the county of Stirling. He married Isabella Monteith, daughter of William Monteith, Esq., who survives him, and was succeeded by his only son.

8. James Stirling of Garden. Mr. Stirling was born in 1844, and succeeded to his estate about a year ago.

THE FORRESTERS OF ARNGIBBON.

THE estate of Arngibbon is pleasantly situated near the village of Arnprior, and adjoins the property of Garden. The mansion-house is built on a commanding eminence, having a sweeping view of the vale of Monteith, the eastern portion of the Lennox, with the whole range of the Grampian hills beyond. The present beautiful house was built and the grounds laid out by the esteemed proprietor, which reflects the highest credit on his taste and intelligence. The name of Forrester is of great antiquity, and the family is one of the very oldest, in a direct line, in the county of Stirling. The name is derived from the office of "forester" or "keeper" of the king's forests. The present Mr. Forrester of Arngibbon is descended, in a direct line, from the ancient proprietors of Garden of that name.

Previous to the year 1490, Garden appears to have been crown lands; for, in 1495, Sir Duncan Forrester, who would appear to have been the first laird of Garden of that name, had charters of the lands of Garden, Skipness, Torwood, Torwoodhead, &c.; and was also comptroller of the King's* household, and had the office of keeper of the forest of Torwood. About the year 1613, Sir Andrew Forrester sold

* Note to Douglass Peerage.

his estate of Garden to Stirling of Keir,* but appears to have retained the estate of Arngibbon.

At a very early period, and for a very long time, the Menzies were proprietors of the greater part of the parishes of Kippen and Killearn; and during the reign of James IV. one of that name held the ancient estate of Arnprior. Menzies was an old man without heirs, and had long lived at enmity with Forrester of Garden. The latter being the more powerful of the two continued to overawe his neighbour, and at last brought matters to a crisis by ordering Menzies either to leave his estate voluntarily to him, or he would come and drive him from it by force. Menzies not being able to cope with Garden, but at the same time very unwilling to leave his estate to his mortal enemy, wrote Buchanan of Auchmar that if he would protect him from Garden he would leave the estate to one of his sons. Buchanan readily accepted the offer, and so far undervalued Garden that he sent his second son, then only an infant, with his nurse to Arnprior.

Forrester, hearing of the " young heir," instantly went to Arnprior house, and demanded that he should be at once sent back, otherwise he should kill the child and burn the house about his ears. The nurse, however, being of a bold, determined nature, brandished her fist in Forrester's face, exclaiming—" Touch but one hair of the child's head, and you bring the vengeance of Auchmar upon you; to-morrow, you shall be hanging on your own gibbet, and your estate be a ruin!" This bold speech on the part of the nurse was a complete damper to Forrester, who well knew he could

* Keir Papers.

not cope with the then powerful house of Auchmar, and he ceased to molest his neighbour. This same infant in after life became the renowned " King of Kippen," as the following incident will show:—

During the reign of King James V. carriers were frequently passing along the road, from the western portions of the county, to Stirling, with goods for the King's use, the county road leading past the entrance to Buchanan's house. On one occasion Buchanan ordered the carrier to leave part of the load for his use, and he should be paid for it; but the carrier refusing, Buchanan instantly compelled him to give up what he wanted, telling the bewildered carrier that, if his master was " King of Scotland," he was " King of Kippen," and that it was reasonable he should share with his neighbour King.

. This matter afterwards coming to the ears of James, he resolved on paying Arnprior a visit. On his arrival Buchanan was at dinner, and his Majesty was denied access by a tall fellow, who brandished a battle-axe, and told the King there could be no admittance till dinner was over; but this answer not being satisfactory, the King sent to demand admittance a second time, upon which he was desired by the porter to desist, otherwise he should have cause to repent of his rudeness.

James, finding this method not suitable, desired the porter to tell his master that the " Guid man o' Ballangeich desired to speak with the " King of Kippen." Buchanan hearing this, instantly received his Majesty, entertained him sumptuously; and made himself so agreeable, that he was allowed to take whatever he wanted for his own use out of the King's carts, and desired to visit his Majesty at Stirling, which he did, and continued afterwards in great favour.

This Buchanan of Arnprior was also proprietor of the estate of Gartartan, and had charters from the Commendator of Inchmahome of the lands of Hornhaugh; he was also laird of Brachern. After he had got possession of Brachern, it was violently seized by Captain M'Tormad, chief of a company of outlaws, who took possession and plundered the property.

Buchanan getting notice that M'Tormad and his associates were drinking in a tavern at Chapelarroch near Gartmore, and were likely to spend the night there, selected a number of his men mounted on horseback, and arrived at Chapelarroch during the night. On Buchanan's arrival, he found the outlaws overcome with drink and sleep, and making fast the doors, he set fire to the house, when their chief and his followers, twenty-four in number, were either burned or slain. This brave man, the first of the " Kings of Kippen," was killed at the disastrous battle of Pinkie.*

The estate of Arngibbon is situated in the county of Perth, but the family has always been reckoned as of Stirlingshire.

* Historical Essay upon the Family and Surname of Buchanan, by Buchanan of Auchmar.

THE M'LACHLANS OF AUCHENTROIG.

THE mansion-house of Auchentroig stands in one of the most pleasant situations in the county of Stirling—placed, as it is, on the banks of the pretty little glen of Arnfaichloch, famous in " Border Tales," watered by the meandering stream that flows around it, and adorned with some of the grandest old trees in the country. The present esteemed proprietor has done much for the improvement of the estate and the benefit of his tenantry. The house and grounds, having been built and laid out under his direc-tion, give ample proof of his taste, and of the deep interest he takes in matters agricultural.

The family of Auchentroig have long been distinguished for their liberal spirit, disinterestedness, and noble hospita-lity; while they have always taken a deep interest in every-thing tending to promote the good of the district in which their estate is situated. The family is generally allowed to be one of the very oldest, in a direct line from father to son, in the county of Stirling. I have heard an old friend of mine, long since gathered to his fathers, who was well versed in all the traditions of the family, say that "fourteen Johns succeeded each other in direct succession!" Certain it is, at least, that they have held the property from a very early period.

According to Welsh, the Irish historian, the ancestor of
the M'Lachlans was O'Lauchlan, King of the province of
Meath, and one of the Milesian stem, or race of the ancient
Kings of Ireland, who reigned from the second century
till about the time of the English Conquest, when they
were among the first to plant Argyleshire. An important
branch of the clan held the Auchentroig estate as far back
as the twelfth or thirteenth century. The chief of this
branch led a company of spearmen from his estate, and
swelled the renowned Randolph's division at the battle of
Bannockburn. Charters, granted by King Robert Bruce
after the battle, and still preserved among the Auchentroig
papers, are proofs that he had rendered to his King and
country, on that important day, valuable services. In the
year 1394, Duncan, Earl of Lennox, confirms a charter to
Celestin M'Lachlan of Auchentroig, granted to one of his
ancestors by Eugen M'Kessan of Garchel.*

The late Captain M'Lachlan of Auchentroig, the grandfather of the present proprietor, was a gentleman of very
many accomplishments. In early life he was allowed to
be one of the best swordsmen in the British army, and was
endowed with a singularly daring spirit. On one occasion,
and when only a subaltern, he commanded a picket party,
while, on the opposite side of a ravine, lay a detachment
of the enemy. During the early part of the evening, the
officer in charge of the enemy's party cried, "We'll sort you
lousy Scots to-morrow." "If ye'll see to-morrow!" whispered
the young subaltern. During the night, M'Lachlan led his
men quietly across the glen, and next morning the sun rose

* Essay, by Buchanan of Auchmar.

on the corpses of the entire party of the enemy. For this exploit he was tried next day by court-martial and admonished; but on the following day he had the satisfaction of being raised to the rank of Captain. On a subsequent occasion he engaged a French officer single-handed, when the Frenchman kept backing his horse, till its progress was arrested by a wall; "and then," said the veteran, "I soon laid his head upon his shoulders." Another feat is recorded of his taking a French officer from the very front of his regiment, and carrying him a prisoner to the British lines amid the plaudits of the soldiery. At the battle of Minden, he distinguished himself by carrying off the enemy's colours; but in this gallant act he was unhorsed and severely wounded. On being asked, in afterlife, how he managed to escape after his horse was killed, he replied, "Ah! there were plenty of empty saddles before I left."

He died at Auchentroig, at a good old age, and was succeeded by his only son, the late Captain M'Lachlan, one of the most accomplished gentlemen of his time. In early life he gave tokens of possessing poetical talents of a high order, some of his pieces bearing favourable comparison even with those of our great National Bard; but his unfortunate death, in early life, extinguished all the hopes of his friends.

He was succeeded in the estate by his only son, the present Mr. M'Lachlan of Auchentroig—a gentleman well known in the west of Stirlingshire for his many good qualities, and the deep interest he takes in all that tends to the advancement of his native district.

A SABBATH ON BEN-LOMOND.

IT is a Saturday afternoon, early in summer. We are leaving the Port of Monteith station, with the grave intention of "doing" (as the Cockneys call it) Ben-Lomond on Sunday morning. Our clerical friends may call this Sabbath desecration, or anything else they choose —no matter. Here we are, rolling along the Forth & Clyde Railway towards Balloch; and, sweeping through the grand old country of the Lennox, we reach the foot of Loch-Lomond in time for the last boat to take us up the loch. As we set foot on board, a gentle breeze is sweeping down from the mountains, and ruffling the hitherto still waters of the Queen of Scottish Lakes. As our gallant craft ploughs the blue waters, and steers her course among riven rocks and feathered islands, our eye scans the distant shores where rise modern mansion and ancient feudal keep—the home of the merchant prince, and the abode of the war chief of other days. We see the pine-covered glens and barren mountain gorges, where, in days long gone by, the Macfarlane, Macaulay, and Colquhoun rushed forth, like their native torrents, to rob the plain, their faces tatooed with the scars of a hundred battles, and their limbs red with blood, as they mingled in fray and foray, and wreaked vengeance on the Buchanan.

We reach Rowardennan just as the sun is sinking behind the hills, and day beginning to wane in the glens of the country of Rob Roy; and, after refreshing ourselves on the good things of the inn, we stroll along the shore, to muse on Nature's glories, and inhale the balmy breeze of loch and hill. Slowly we tread the rugged beach, and examine the rocks smoothed by the waves of a thousand years, and grooved by the surge of icebergs of countless ages. All is still in the Highland glen, but ever and anon we are startled by the dismal wail of the owl, as it floats down the pass, or the cry of the sea-bird, as it returns from the feeding haunts away to its young on yonder island. By-and-by, night throws her sable garb around the hills, and the mist wades among the stinted hazels and creeps over the morass; while the moon, like an ill-washed face, peeps over the heathery knowe. We retire to rest;—and at the first streak of day we are at the window peering through the gloom. But alas! the mist is far down on the mighty object of our ambition, the winds howl, and the window-curtains rattle; while the loch, like an angry beast, with breath of hate and tongue of foam, growling laps the shore, and, dull and disappointed, we creep back to our couch, and spend an hour or two more in dreamy repose.

By-and-by, we hear the old Highland clock strike three; when we again start to our feet, and rush towards the window. Now we find that the wind has stopped its raving, the curtains ceased to rattle, and the loch, no longer angry, playfully kisses the pebbles on the beach; while far between us and the blue vaulted heavens, Ben-Lomond, with clear head and frownless brow, looks down on the scene beneath. In every glen, bird sings to bird, rock and corry yielding back the chorus; while the glorious orb of day, uprisen from his hiding-place, is dotting the shattered hills with his tints, and filling each rugged glen with a flood of light. A few moments longer, sandwich in bag and flask in hand, we are treading the heather on towards the summit. The first mile, we find, somewhat resembles the journey of life, being largely composed of "ups and downs," and not particularly interesting; but as we gradually ascend and pass on to the second mile, reaching a point where "Providence" has kindly "dug" a well, the scene deepens, and we have a beautiful view of the lower and broader portion of the loch.

The sun is just high enough to peep over the shoulder of yon neighbouring crag, and as it flings its first rays over tinted, deep, and shaggy islands, we find we are gazing upon a scene perhaps unsurprised in all Nature's glories. The whole lower portion lies spread out before us, calm and shining like a vast mirror—the islands reposing on its surface,—while all seems a diadem in Nature's lap. We are struck with the great diversity of shape and colour as they nestle in the morning sun; some with rocky face and heath-covered head shoot high in the air, their sides clothed with flowing birch and stately pine, stunted oak and rank fern, throwing their dark shadows far across the loch; others, with rocky surface and craggy headland, seem bleak and barren; while here and there may be seen reposing low-shaped green islands, almost covered by the tiny waves that play around them, and lying on the blue waters like so many emeralds. It is with difficulty we tear ourselves

N

away from the enjoyment of such a scene; but as the hill-top is free of mist and clear of cloud, we push on upwards —still upwards. As we tread over barren rock and stunted heather, we see the gull and the falcon hunting hill and glen, while the raven breaks the air with his cries, as he wheels in grand circles over our head.

By-and-by we reach the summit, and the glorious scene that bursts upon our awe-struck vision will haunt our memory and float before our imagination till our dying day. On either side, rise the scattered glories of the great Creator; beneath, are the glens of the nether world, dark and gloomy as they appear. Around, we see mountain rise over mountain in sublime magnificence; there, huge dark forms splintered into a thousand shapes. There, too, lies the sweeping plain, dotted with loch and watered by river; yonder the smiling Lowland village and snug Highland hamlet; beyond, the great City, where commerce rolls her busy tide, discernible only by the dim pall of smoke that throws its sable tresses over it. Towards the west, we have the hills of Arrochar, with ever and anon a peep of Loch-Long between. Conspicuous among the hills stands the "Cobler," with furrowed face and bent back; farther north, Ben-Voirlich (Ben-Lomond's twin brother) rears his noble head. Sweeping along the northern horizon our eyes rests on the proud summits of Ben-Cruachan, Ben-More, and Ben-Lawers, with a thousand hills between. On the east, we have the hills that overawe Loch-Katrine; with the Alpine ranges of Loch-Tay and Loch-Earn in the back-ground. Towards the south, we have the Vale of Monteith, with its varied landscape; while Loch-Chon, Loch-Ard, and the Lake of

Monteith lie slumbering beneath heathery hills, and shaded by golden-tinted foliage. Beyond, in one unbroken plain, stretches the Carse of Stirling, with the Castle rock and Abbey Craig rising through the haze; while far beyond is the sea-girt shore of the Frith of Forth. From beneath our feet spring innumerable tiny rills, which, strengthened by the streams that gurgle from the parent hill—like blood from wounded giant's side—and pours forth their waters, that in the plain become rivers, and swell out into billowy seas.

While enraptured we stand gazing on the wonderful panorama before us, we are startled by a low sort of playfully prattling noise; and on looking round we find that the summer cloud is fast gathering beyond, and that the mist is coming hissing up the hill-side. Watching it, as it comes rushing through the riven crags, it reminds one of some half-dozen urchins climbing up their grandfather's old rickety chair, each trying who will be first to place his tiny hand on the bald head. Upwards still climbs the fog, and in a moment we are enveloped in impenetrable gloom. By-and-by the mist settles down; and, starting to our feet, a sense of awful loneliness steals over us. We imagine ourselves some sea-bird perched on lonely rock, and far from shore; for, far as the eye can reach there is mist—only mist, with here and there the top of some mountain piercing the thick veil—like islands in a vast sea.

' Soon a gentle breeze springs up from the north—and, in a thousand forms, back is rolled the sable mantle; then, bursting through the shattered folds emerges the sun—and, shining through the watery vapour, spans the neighbouring hill-top with a rainbow most beautiful to behold. As we viewed the scenes as they passed before us with mingled feelings of pleasure and awe, we felt a hallowed sensation thrill through our souls, as if we had left mortality behind us, and had plucked a feather out of seraphic wing.

A BUCHLYVIE LYKE-WAKE OF THE OLDEN
TIME.

THE days of "Lyke or Late Wakes" have in a great
measure gone by, and although they are still kept up in
certain rural districts, the debauches and orgies of yore
have happily passed away.

In farm and cottars' houses, when the remains of the
deceased cannot be secured from the inroads of vermin,
it may perhaps become a matter of expediency to "wake"
in such cases; but this is now done by a few friends of
the family in a quiet and becoming manner. It was not
so, however, about the beginning of the present century,
or even at a much later period. The scene here detailed
was often described by an old friend of mine who lived in
the immediate neighbourhood; and at the time it occurred,
such scenes were by no means rare, although, perhaps,
none so wild or devilish in their nature.

It was at the fall of the year, when fields are bare, the
corn all gathered in, and when the old bodies begin to
drop away one by one; when the sharp hoar-frost strews
the ground with falling leaves, and the gusts of wind begin
to wreck nature, and send wanderers running to their
homes. November had set in, with its surly blasts blow-
ing straight from Ben-Ledi—that mother of frosts; and

poor bodies, with their thin clothes, thin flesh, and far
thinner blood, could ill stand the shock. The link that
bound them to earth was shivered; and so it was with the
taxman of Upper Kepdourie. He was honest, true, and
old; he had

> " Seen yon weary wintry sun
> Twice forty times return;
> And every time had added proofs
> That man was made to mourn."

When the " word broke out" that the old man had died,
servant-maids and " herd laddies" might be seen meeting
at the marches, and laying schemes for the wake. " It'll
be a guid ane," one would say. " Ye'll be there," another
would whisper. " We'll ha'e a nicht o't—the auld wife's a
hearty ane." " Ay, feth!" And so they whiled away the time
till it turned dark. The old man died in the morning;
and in the fore part of the day the wind began to blow the
leaves into eddies at the roadsides, the afternoon was
drizzling and wet, and with the dark came the piercing
storm. The sleet drifted along the braes of Buchlyvie;
the burns began to come down; and the spate roared
among the rocks of Arnfaichlach glen. The wind howled
among the turrets of the old baronial house of Auchentroig,
and soughed wildly among the dark recesses of " Garry's
Hole;" and, in fact, it was such a night

> " That a child might understand
> The de'il had business on his hand."

In spite, however, of drifting sleet and splashy road, the
wakers began to gather. The farmer left his horse and
kine to pay the last tribute of respect to his honest neigh-

bour; the country weaver left his shuttle mute, and hurried through the drift to lend his presence to the scene;
the cobbler and tailor flung aside the awl and needle to
"wake" their honest friend; while Vulcan rushed from
din of hammer, steekit the smithy door, and groped his
way in the dark along a road famous in days of yore for
the haunts of spirits and the resort of ghosts, to lend con-
solation to the lonely widow.

It was an old custom, and a good one, at scenes of this
kind, that when the "wakers" first arrived, each had to
drink a large horn of whisky, and on this occasion it was
not overlooked. We shall now suppose the company to
be assembled; and the gentle reader will please follow me
while I describe the house, that he may have a better idea
how matters went on. The little farm-house of Upper
Kepdourie was one of those old-fashioned one-storeyed
"biggins," with a "but and ben," and small closet; the
kitchen was large and roomy, with a bed near the back
wall, and close to the "bed-end" was the back window.

In front of the house there was a "causeway," made up
of rough stones, and only about three or four feet wide;
beyond this was the manure-stead, which, when filled with
the sap of the dung, was from four to six feet in depth. As
Fate would have it, the farmer's old mare chanced to die
the same day as her master, and still lay unburied within
the stable, which stood but a few yards from the kitchen
door. Some wags had laid their heads together during the
day, and resolved to have some fun at the wakers' expense.
Getting access to the house during the day, they fixed a
rope round the neck of the corpse, concealing it with the bed-

clothes, and had it drawn out at the window, to be ready
when the convenient time arrived. With some labour, but
aided by the stormy night and the din within, they managed
to drag the dead animal unheard to the front of the kitchen
door, and fixed on its back, the four legs grimly dangling in
the air. Placed in this position, no one could get out without falling over the hideous carcase, and once over, they
were sure to get buried in the " wash." This part of the
performance over, the lads stood by the rope and waited
their time, seeing and hearing all that passed within.
Gathered around the blazing peat fire sat the wakers, a
rather motley crew, old and young, lads and lasses. At one
side sat the weaver and his friend the cobbler, discussing
the news and events of the times; at the other, sat two
farmer chiels, cracking about " horse," and swearing; while
in the peat-neuk sat two herd laddies, bragging who had the
best roaring bull or fighting dog; and in each corner were
lads with their arms around the lasses' necks. In front
of the fire, stood a large four-footed table, groaning with
bottles, and reeking with hot punch; at the head was the
" big bowl"—dear to the old man as the " big ha' Bible,"
and far dearer to the wakers. Near the head of the table
sat the douce old widow, in her drugget clothes and snow-
white " sou-back" cap; at her side was the grey, lank, lean
smith, but yaul for his age, his great fists like " fore-ham-
mers," and the big blue veins twisted round his arms like
" ivy stems on oaks." The smith had a singular gift for
seeing ghosts, and a wonderful knack of telling ghost
stories. He was a great favourite with the widow, and
between rounds of punch they " cracked" loud and long.

" Ye ha'e met wi' a serious loss, and I'm unco vexed to hear o' the death o' yer guid mare," whispered the smith to the widow; "and," continued he, "mony a time I ha'e pit shin on her feet."

" Ou ay, deed ha'e ye, smith. It's a great loss to me the loss o' my gallant mare;—the guidman, ye ken, was gettin' a wee doited—it was just natur failin'," responded the widow.

" Bodies, be hearty," cried the old dame, turning round in her rickety chair. "Smith, gi'e them a drap o't, it's guid speerits; an' atween you and me, smith, it ne'er saw the face o' a gauger." "Lassock," she continued, "see that that licht's no gaun din on the guidman's breast; the witches would turn him in a moment; I ance had a forebearer that was couped, an' them a' i' the house! Lord help us! it was awfu'!"

"But, smith," whispered the widow, "I was hearin' ye got a bit glif o' our auld neebor, Mungo, the ither nicht?"

" Atweel awat, I did that," responded the smith. " I was jist takin' a bit dauner i' the gloamin', the ither nicht, an', comin' near the tree* he planted wi' his ain haun, and who should I see but himsel', dressed in his auld red nicht-cap and blue breeks; an' vera sin'glar, woman, he was sittin' on his ain barra that wheel'd hame his corpse, and lookin' wi' a waefu' look up to yon big branch that's neist Garbawn. I was jist openin' my mouth to say 'Is that you, Mungo?' when awa he flew."

---

* " Mungo's Tree," on the roadside, a little below the Station of Buchlyvie, and where, it is said, a man of the name of " Mungo," after planting the tree, hung himself on one of its branches. Of course, the quarter is still haunted by his ghost!

"Ou ay, smith," returned the old dame; "he'll no get rest in his grave; he took awa his ain life, ye ken, and atweel awat he needna fash'd, he wudna ha'e been lang hinner'd at ony rate."

By this time the drink had done its own work; the lads and lasses made grand sport in the corners, while peats and potatoes were showered through the house like hail. The smith began to make an awful noise among the glasses, and to boast about his courage and strength; and, in fact,

> " The mirth and fun flew fast and furious."

The whole affair collapsed when Vulcan struck the table a blow with his mighty fist that made it shiver on its legs; and, springing to his feet, with a voice like an echo, he drank the health of the departed, while the whole house rose to do it honours. The rascals at the rope saw their time was now come, and pulling gently till they got the body nearly in an upright position, then giving a tremendous jerk, they sent the old farmer right into the midst of the floor!

There was a moment of terrible stillness—then a wild roar and a rush to get out,—while the smith gave a fearful look, opened his lank jaws, and pronounced a word awfully like " hell," and dashed towards the door howling—"O Lord! it's Auld Nick's wark!"

> " Then backward quick the door he drew,
> And forward o'er the horse he flew;
> One by one they on did dash,
> O'er head and heels among the wash
> Some roared out good, but more did evil,
> While Vulcan yelled 'It's sure the devil!'
> He felt his rough and shaggy hide,
> For o'er his belly he did glide.

The weaver he did roar and wail,
As sure as death he saw the tail;
It was a short and hairy stump,
For o'er the hind legs he did thump,
And by the heels as he played bag,
The horrid thing it gie'd a wag!"

CURIOUS OLD TRADITION REGARDING THE
EARL OF MONTEITH.

ON some occasion, when one of the Earls of Monteith was entertaining his friends on the island, he accidentally ran short of wine. On finding out the mistake, he ordered his butler to set off to Stirling with all speed, and to lose no time in returning with the required "material." The servant instantly set off on the mission, but hour after after fled on; and no word of the butler or wine, until at last the guests had to retire minus their tumblers. Enraged at the delay, early next morning the Earl walked into the servants' hall, to learn whether the butler had yet arrived; and on entering the apartment he found the truant fast asleep on a bench, with the barrel beside him. The enraged nobleman instantly roused and chid him for his negligence. "Pardon me, my Lord," exclaimed the butler, as he scratched his matted locks, and rubbed his half-open eyes—"I have been for wine, and if I mistake not, have brought you the best that ever was in your cellar. When near the shore of the lake, I spied two honest women, each mounted on a bulrush, and crying to each other, 'Ha'e wi' you, Marion Bowie!' 'Ha'e wi' you, Elspa Hardie!' 'Ha'e wi' you too!' says I, mounting like them on a bulrush. Instantly we were rushing through the regions of space, and immediately found ourselves in the palace of the King of France. As for myself, I was near a sideboard, where there was a store of wine, and, being invisible to the people, I took the opportunity of filling your Lordship's cask. I have also found the cup out of which his Imperial Majesty was wont to drink. I then returned on my trusty nag as quickly as I went; and here I am again, my Lord, at your Lordship's pleasure." During dinner the company were delighted with the fine character of the wines, and not a little amazed on hearing the Earl tell the way in which it had been procured. The story was confirmed when the Earl called his butler, and made him show to the company "the elegant silver cup on which was engraved the fleur-de-lis of the House of Bourbon!"

CURIOUS TRADITION REGARDING THE FAIRIES.

On the south-eastern shore of the lake of Monteith there is a singular peninsula called Cnoc-n'an-Bocan, "Bogle-knowe," or "Hobgoblin-hill," and which was the head-quarters of "all the fairies" in this district of country. During the time these "lubberly supernaturals" held the "Cnoc-n'an-Bocan," the then Earls of Monteith possessed what was called the "red book," to open which was to be followed by something preternatural. One of the Earls unfortunately unclasped the fatal volume, when, lo! the fairies appeared before him demanding work. Not know-ing what work to set them to, his lordship hit upon the plan of making a road into the island. They began on the southern shore, and had made the now beautiful and pleasing peninsula of "Arnmauk," tufted with its dark green Scotch firs. The Earl, however, finding that if they continued this work his hitherto impregnable retreat would be cut off, asked them to make for him a rope of sand. They began this latter task without finishing the former, and finding their new work too much for them, they resolved to depart, to the no small joy of the Earl. His lordship, however, in consideration of their herculean toils, unfinished as they were, gave them a grant of the north shoulder of Ben-Venue, still called Coir-n'an-Uriskin.

M'Gregor Stirling says, "To their desire for work may be attributed the vegetable splendour of their present abode, which without it would have had the most forlorn aspect imaginable, but adorned as it now is, presents unequalled specimens of the sublime and beautiful conjoined. There is, indeed, in Coir-n'an-Uriskin and Bealoch-n'an-Bo, a certain magic grace bespeaking the aerial tenantry." Coir-n'an-Uriskin is the cove of the "Urisk's" or "Fairies," Bealoch-n'an-Bo, the "Lass of the Cows."

MONTEITH—EARL OF MONTEITH.

THE first possessor of this very ancient and extensive Earldom appears to have been—

Murdoch Monteith, who is first mentioned in the chartulary of Dunfermline in the reign of David I.

2. He was succeeded by Gilchrist Monteith, who is mentioned in a charter of donation to the monastery of Scone by Malcolm IV.

3. He was succeeded by Mauritius, Earl of Monteith, who flourished about the time of William I., and is witness to a donation of William Cumyn, Earl of Buchan, to the monastery of Cambuskenneth. He died leaving two daughters.

4. The eldest daughter married Walter Cumyn, Lord of Badenoch, who succeeded to the Earldom in right of his wife. He held extensive tracts of land in Badenoch, and became one of the most influential men of his time, owing as much to the strength of his talents as the number of his vassals in Badenoch and Monteith. He died an old man in 1258, leaving no male issue.

His Countess having married an obscure Englishman, the Earldom devolved upon Walter Stewart, brother of the High Steward of Scotland, who was married to the youngest daughter.

5. This Walter Stewart, who is described in a former article, had two sons, who assumed the surname of Monteith, but the family retained the paternal coat of Stewart,* altering the fesse to a bend for difference.

1. Alexander, sixth Earl of Monteith.

2. Sir John Monteith *alias* "the fause Monteith," the betrayer of Sir William Wallace, and mentioned in a former article.

Sir John Monteith had three sons—important men of their time.

1. Sir Walter Monteith, who had a charter of the lands of "Thora," in the Earldom of Monteith.

2. Sir John Monteith, who had charters from King Robert I. of the lands of Stragartenay, in Perthshire.

3. Sir Alexander Monteith, who had a charter from David II. of the pasturage of 100 cattle and 300 sheep on his Majesty's moors of Carale, in Fife.

5. Alexander, sixth Earl of Monteith, the eldest son, was one of the leaders of the Scotch army which invaded Cumberland in March of the year 1296. He was afterwards taken prisoner by the English at the battle of Dunbar, in April of the same year. He died about the year 1230, leaving two sons.

1. Alan, seventh Earl of Monteith.

2. Murdoch, eighth Earl of Monteith.

6. Alan, seventh Earl of Monteith, had a son and daughter. The son, however, appears to have died before his father, and without issue.

Murdoch, eighth Earl of Monteith, succeeded his brother

* Douglas Peerage.

O

Alan, the seventh Earl, but, being killed at the battle of Halidonhill, 19th July 1333, left no issue.

7. Mary, Countess of Monteith, daughter of Earl Alan, now succeeded to the Earldom. She married Sir John Graham, who, in right, became Earl of Monteith. He was taken prisoner at the battle of Durham in 1346, but having previously sworn fealty to Edward, he was shortly after executed as a traitor, leaving by his Countess one daughter.

8. Margaret, Countess of Monteith, carried the Earldom to her husband, Robert Stewart, third son of King Robert II., Earl of Fife and Duke of Albany, Regent of Scotland. After the execution of her son Murdo, Duke of Albany, the Earldom vested in the crown in the year 1425; but, two years later, it was granted to Malise Graham, Earl of Strathearn, who laid the succession to the Earldom of the name of Graham.

GRAHAM—EARL OF MONTEITH.

1. Malise Graham, Earl of Monteith, appears to have been the only son of Patrick, Earl of Strathearn. The King having divested him of the Earldom of Strathearn, gave him that of Monteith. It does not appear that he was a man of any note. He died about the year 1491. He married Lady Ann Vere, daughter of the Earl of Oxford, and had issue three sons:—

1. Alexander.

2. Sir John Graham of Kilbride. This Sir John was known as "Sir John of the bright sword;" he held, from his father, charters of the lands of Port, Coldon, Monievrachie, "with the Loch of Inchmahome and the Islands thereof." He was ancestor of the Grahams of Gartmore, Preston, Netherby, Norton, Conyers, &c.*

3. Walter, ancestor of the Grahams of Buchquhaple. He held the lands of Lochton, Glaskelgie, Colyart, &c.; he had also charters of several lands in Monteith, with the Lake of Loch-Chon.

1. Alexander, Master of Monteith, died before his father, leaving one son.

3. Alexander, second Earl of Monteith, was served heir

* Douglas Peerage.

to his grandfather, 6th May 1493. He married a daughter of Buchanan of Buchanan, and had issue two sons:—

1. William, third Earl of Monteith.

2. Walter, who had a charter of the lands of Gartur from the Abbot of Inchmahome, and was ancestor of the Grahams of Gartur.

4. William, third Earl of Monteith, died in 1537. He married a daughter of Mubray of Barnbougle, by whom he had issue three sons and one daughter.

1. John, fourth Earl of Monteith.

2. Robert, who got the estate of Gartmore, but died without issue.

3. Gilbert, who appears to have got the Gartmore estate on the death of his brother, but whose male line became extinct.

Lady Margaret, married to the Earl of Argyll.

5. John, fourth Earl of Monteith, appears to have been a man of some note. He was taken prisoner at the "rout of Solway," and was afterwards killed in a duel by the Tutor of Appin in 1547. He married a daughter of Lord Seton, and had issue two sons and two daughters:—

1. William, fifth Earl of Monteith.

2. George Graham, who had the estate of Rednock; he had a son, James, who held a charter of the King's lands of Easter Rednock. James had one daughter, Marion, who was heiress to her grandfather, George. She married John Graham of Duchray, and conveyed the estate to her husband.

1. Lady Mary, who married the Laird of Buchanan.

2. Lady Christian, who married Sir William Livingston of Kilsyth.

6. William, fifth Earl of Monteith, married the eldest daughter of Sir James Douglas of Drumlanrig, and had issue one son.

7. John, sixth Earl of Monteith, was served heir to his father in 1587, and died 1598. He married Mary, third daughter of Sir Colin Campbell of Glenurchy, by whom he had issue two sons and one daughter.

1. William, seventh Earl of Monteith.

2. Hon. Sir James Graham, who married Lady Margaret Erskine, daughter of the Earl of Buchan. They had a daughter married to Walter Graham of Gartur.

Lady Christian, married to Sir John Blackadder of Tulliallan.

8. William, seventh Earl of Monteith, succeeded to the Earldom in the year 1610. In August 1630 he was served heir of David, Earl of Strathearn, and was designed "Earl of Strathearn and Monteith." Earl William appears to have been a man of transcendent genius. The great superiority of his talents attracted the notice of Charles I., and that monarch promoted him to the high offices of Justice-General of Scotland and President of the Privy-Council, and he held charters of extensive lands and baronies. Being a man of great ambition, and having a pedigree reaching back to David, Earl of Strathearn, eldest son of King Robert II., the King and his ministers for Scotland soon began to view him with jealousy, heightened by a diversity of opinion regarding the legitimacy of King Robert II., thereby affecting Charles' right to the throne—a man who, in the opinion of many, had the preferable right to the crown. The Earl at last brought down upon himself the displeasure of his

monarch by exclaiming, in his presence, " My blood is the reddest in the kingdom." Charles at once ordered a reduction of his retours, deprived him of the Justice-Generalship, and set aside his patent as Earl of Strathearn. The King, however, was some short time afterwards pleased to confer upon him the new title of Earl of Airth, and he was afterwards known as Earl of Airth and Monteith. He got a new investiture of the lands of Monteith, granted under the great seal, 11th January 1644, to himself and his son John, Lord Kinpont, as heir-apparent.* He married a daughter of Lord Gray, and had issue four sons and three daughters.

1. John, Lord Kinpont.

2. The Hon. Sir Charles Graham, who died without issue.

3. The Hon. Sir James Graham, who also died without issue.

4. The Hon. Archibald Graham, who had one son by his wife, Janet Johnston; whose male line, however, appears to have become extinct previous to the death of the last Earl.

1. Lady Mary, who married Sir John Campbell of Glenurchy, and was mother of the first Earl of Breadalbane.

2. Lady Margaret, who married Lord Garlies.

3. Lady Anne, married to Sir Mungo Murray of Blebo.

2. John, Lord Kinpont, the eldest son and heir-apparent of William, Earl of Airth and Monteith, had charters of the lands of Kilbride and Kinpont. His Lordship appears to have been a man of great interest and ability, and a keen royalist. He joined his noble chief, the renowned

* Peerage of Scotland.

Marquis of Montrose, with 400 of his followers, taking a prominent part in the decisive battle of Tippermuir, fought on the 1st September 1644, and where Montrose gained a complete victory over an army quadruple in numbers. Four days afterwards, Lord Kinpont was basely murdered in Montrose's camp, at Collare, in Perthshire, by James Stewart of Ardvoirlich. It would appear that Stewart had proposed a plan to his Lordship to assassinate Montrose, whereupon Lord Kinpont at once signified his abhorrence of the act as being " disgraceful and devilish." Stewart, afraid of discovery, without saying a word drew his dagger and stabbed him to the heart, and immediately fled over to the Covenanters. The Marquis of Montrose was deeply affected by the loss of his noble friend, and ordered his body to be conveyed to Monteith, and there interred within the family burying-vault. His Lordship married Lady Mary Keith, by whom he had issue.

1. William, second Earl of Airth and Monteith.
2. Mary, married to Sir John Alardice of Alardice.
3. Elizabeth, married to Sir William Graham of Gartmore.
4. William, second Earl of Airth and Monteith, succeeded his grandfather in the title and estate. He does not appear to have been a man of any note, or to have taken any part in public affairs. Dying without issue, on the 12th of September 1694, he bequeathed all his landed property to the Marquis of Montrose, and the moveable to Sir John Graham of Gartmore. He married, first, Anne Hews; and secondly, Catherine, second daughter of Thomas Bruce of Blairhall, in Perthshire, who pre-deceased him.

EXTRACTS FROM THE RECORD OF THE
SESSION-BOOK OF PORT.*

The oldest is dated "The 14 off Septr. 1664," and is as follows:—"My Lord Bishop of Dunblane preached after our minister's death." "The last of Aprill 1665, the dean preached and held Session."

"The 2d of June 1665 the clerk gat to the presbyterie, and gatt nothing ffor his pains, these severall tymes."

"The 25 of June, Donald Stewartt, Andrew Donaldsone, Duncan Fishar, Alexander Monteath, Wm. M'Callen, went to the bishop to supplicat him for a minister, and they got — sh. Scots for yer expences."

"The 27 August, Mr. Bowere, dean of Edinburgh, preached."

"The 30 day of Sepr the Bishop preached."

"The 22d of Janry' 1667, Sir William Graham of Gartmore had ane child babtised, called John. Witness, Thos. Graham in Monduy and —— M'Lachlan." (This was Sir John Graham the second and last Baronet of Gartmore.)

"The 14th February' 1667, David Lord Cardross had ane child babtized, called Madelen."

"The 15 off August, Mr. William Wymes preached. The

* Copied from Mr. M'Gregor Stirling's work on Inchmahome.

session in regard that there are persons without testimonil comet to the paroch, the session has ordained that such persons be excepted under the pain of twentie pounds Scotts.".

" The 15 off November, the said day James Donaldson was admitted minister of the church."

" The 17 off Nowember the said day Mr James Donaldson preached, being the first day after his admisione." .

" The 1 of Decer the said day Mr James held session being the first session. The session has considered the abuse of the people in standing furth in tym of divyn service. The Session has ordained that Andrew Gyloch, Andrew Donaldson, go furth and search the ale houses, that no persons drink in tym of divyn service, and the minister to nominat the samen to them out of the pulpit; and whosoever shall be found guiltie after intimation made, shall be punished accordinglie, and trio of elders to go Sunday about, and them that comes in after the hinmost bell, to sit bare headit before the minr."

"The 29 of December 1667, compeared Duncan Graham, and humbled himself for breaking the act in coming in after the hinmost bell and confessed his sin, and promised that he should not doo the lyk againe. The session hes ordaint that everie person that bees bookit, shall consigne a dollor and no other thing but money, and gev in caise the on parttie be without the paroche, both are to consign a dollor, and the money to lye for three quarter off a year after the marriage; and giv the woman be with child, boths the dollor are left before marriage, and giv one off them goes bak parted fairlie will loose his dollor, and the partie absserver is to get his." . .

"The 12 dy off Janry' 1668, the said day Pat M'Callen stood publikly befor the congregation for doing the fauld of staying out till after the bell, on his knees was absolved."

" The 20th off Janrÿ 1688, the session hes ordaint Margt. M'Carturt, Janet Giloch, and Wm. M'Ewan, to sit before the minister before the pulpit, and to ansr the minister when they are called upon for their coming to the church in the afternoon aft the last bell."

"The 16 off Febrie, After calling on the name of the Lord, the session has enacted and ordained, that there shall be no drinking after sermon except of necessitee and men be thirsty, that they drink onlie a chopin of ell, or the man serve persons or strangers that comes out of ither parts."

" The 23 off Febrie 1668, After calling on the name of the Lord, the session has ordained that two of the elders goo furth everie Sunday about, that they let non of the people goo away without a lawful excuse. The session, to their serious consideration; considered the horribl sins and great abuses that ordinarilie in all places, experience the sin of drunkeness and comoning on the Lord's day, Therefor the session has acted and ordained, that no bear nor ell seller within the paroch shall sell ell after sermon; except in case of necessitie, folks be thirstie or fant; they drink a chapon of ell, or those that are sick or those that are strangers."

"The 22 of March 1668, The session has ordained John Battison to go and poynd Alex Hardie, and the poynd to be worth 4 lbs: Scots."

" The 23d March 1668, John Pattison went according

to order, and finding nothing in the house but an old ax, returned without any poind."

"The session holden the 5 of April 1668. The session has ordained to give an half-mark to the smith for ane em; ordains to make a leg to the joges."

"On the 26 of April 1668, the qlk day the session convened, all the elders being present except Patrick Ferguson who sent his excuse that he could not come for pain of leg, Archd. Graham, son of the deceyst erlle of Airth, who waited on the west end, and Patrick Morrison waited on the way to Cardross, report to the session that non at all went from the church of Port at the fyrst sermon, and Gilbert Graham, who waited at the est end, reported non got away, save some people of the paroch of Kincarn."

"The session finding, by their former and renewed act, inhibiting all drinking after both sermons endit, save of a chopin of ell drinking and that onlie to be taken in case of necessitie, that they have no ways compassed that great design which they had of suppressing that old sin and scandal of this paroch, of drinking the wholl Lord's day; out of their zeal against the profanatione of the Lord's day, and for the keeping it the more hollie, have ordained that there sall be no drinking at all after both sermons ended, except persons be seik, or it be strangers, and then they not to pass soberlie beyond this, under the pain of ten pounds Scots, to be payit the aille seller in case the violat this act; and the persons drinking to make publick satisfaction therefor, befor the congregatione, and further to be punished cordinglie in their persons and means as the session shall think fit. And for this effect it is ordained that everie elder after both sermons endit, do search for drinking, the respective aille houses within their several quarters."

"The said day, compeared Walter Laganach, John Ure, Patrick M'Cadem, who being proceeded against for drinking on the Sabbath day, being the twelve of April, acknowledge that they were in John M'Culloch's until the sun was neir set, but that they onlie drank a chapon of aill the hand, who was therefore ordained by the minister and session, the next Lord's day to sit bair headit beffor the pulpit, and after sermon endit to acknowledge their scandal on their knees."

"On the 3d of May 1668, The said day the minister did publiclie desire and requested the elders, according to the order of the session, to insist that no brewer within the paroch should sell no aille to no person except alls much as wauld quench the thirst of strangers or to seik persons, and no to sell no aill to no either person within the paroch, and that under the paine of ten pounds Scotts, to be payit be the ail seller, and the person who drink it to be punished as the session shall think fit. He lykwys did intimate unto the people after the first sermon; and intreated them that no person shauld flyt nor scald on the Sabbath day, or no ither day, or whosoever person or persons should be scolding should be punished both in their persons and means and to stand in the Jogs."

"This session has acted and ordained that no parishoner goe in with a stranger after the afternoon sermon to drink in ane alle houss."

"At Port, June 1, 1704, being Thursday, sederunt, the minister and all the elders. After prayer, the session considering that there is a scandalous practice frequently used in the parisch at publick marriages, in the time, and immediately after the solemnization therefore, by the parties there using of charms and inchantments and that notwithstanding they have been sharply and openly rebuked for the same by using circular motions &c; wherefore the session, for preventing this abominable and heathenish practice in all time coming, do statute and ordain, that whosoever shall be found guilty of such a scandalous practice, shall be oblidged to appear publickly before the congregation, and be rebuked for the foresaid guilt, and oppoins the said act to be publickly read the next Lord's day."

Hedderwick & Son, Printers to the Queen.

c

Lightning Source UK Ltd.
Milton Keynes UK
UKHW020734140922
408851UK00005B/547